Soccer
THE GREAT ONES

In the same series
General Editor: John Arlott

*

CRICKET: THE GREAT ONES
CRICKET: THE GREAT BOWLERS
GOLF: THE GREAT ONES (Ben Wright)
CRICKET: THE GREAT ALL-ROUNDERS
Other volumes are being planned

Soccer

THE GREAT ONES

*Studies of Eight
Great Football Players*

*

GENERAL EDITOR

John Arlott

PELHAM BOOKS

First published in Great Britain by
PELHAM BOOKS LTD
26 Bloomsbury Street
London, W.C.1
1968

© *1968 by Bagenal Harvey Organisation*

7207 0201 1

Set and printed in Great Britain by
Tonbridge Printers Ltd, Peach Hall Works, Tonbridge, Kent
in Times ten on twelve point, and bound by
James Burn at Esher, Surrey

PREFACE

There is a tendency in some quarters nowadays to believe – or at least to imply – that British football has only reached a high level in the past decade with a resultant discounting of the play and players of earlier times. This is a serious misunderstanding and under-rating of a game which was developed in this country from a primitively crude, hacking scramble to a sport of high skill.

It is true that, in the nineteen-fifties, the general public in Britain suddenly awakened to the fact, which the experts had seen as unmistakably foreshadowed during the thirties, that European and South American football had reached a higher level of performance than its British parent. That defeat of England, by Hungary, at Wembley in 1953, was not merely a salutary corrective to those who had closed their eyes to the overseas results of the previous twenty years, it also provoked a violent reaction which involved a revulsion against British football of the past. Then, when England won the World Cup in 1966, the people who had taken that violently anti-past view, seemed to accept that our game had reached the top level *for the first time*. That ignores the fact that, for decades, Britain was so supreme in the game that matches against nations outside the Home Countries tournament were regarded as so unimportant that, often half strength – or even weaker – elevens were fielded against them, and until lately 'caps' for those matches were regarded as significantly lower in value than those won against the Home Countries.

Indeed those early, missionary, English teams gained many pathetically easy wins, sometimes by double figures. In that context, incidentally, it is worth noting that, even in 1947, despite the damage our football had suffered during the war, an England eleven beat Portugal, in Lisbon, by 10–0.

What had in fact happened between 1923 and 1953 was that, in overseas countries, the *general* standard of execution of the basic skills had been improved, and team-direction and player-use had

5

been more highly developed. This meant, in effect, that every player in an eleven was likely to be a two-footed master of control; and that the full powers of every member of the team were more completely exploited.

That undoubtedly resulted in a raising of the standards of effectiveness and a widening of those of skill by comparison with those of a day when no one thought of using a full-back as an extra attacker, overlapping down the wing, or of pulling forwards back to help in defence. Above all, the change was from a day when men picked for England might meet their wing partner or full-back colleague for the first time in the dressing-room and, in the absence of any form of management, based their tactics and 'understanding' on a chat while they changed. It is noticeable that the results of the English eleven improved steadily with the growth of team training and discussion under the first two managers ever appointed to the national team – the first of whom, Walter Winterbottom, took as his main aim the development in every player of mastery of the basic skills and the second, Sir Alf Ramsey, concentrated primarily on work-rate. But it may safely be said that, although both saw need for improvement, neither would seriously claim to have lifted the top level of skill. In the field of ability – of power and precision in shooting and heading, accuracy in passing, closeness of control, subtlety of pace or movement with the ball, the great players of the past have not been excelled.

Neither have they been entirely forgotten, for all that there sometimes seems to be a suggestion that the majority of football followers are under twenty-five. In fact, the hard core of support of most clubs – that is to say the people who turn up on cold, wet days and when their side is doing badly – consists of men who can remember at least the immediate post-war game, if not that of the inter-war period. That latter group will recall – from legend if not from actual eye-witness evidence – the famous 'Battle of Highbury' in November 1934 when England beat a murderously inclined Italian side by 3–2, largely through the mighty tackling of Wilf Copping who met violence with old-fashioned, fair – but mighty – tackling.

It is true that few of the players who form the subjects of this book had experience of 4–3–3 or 4–2–4. But who can doubt that they would have met those challenges – or those of the bolt, the retreating defence, or the withdrawn centre-forward with less success than they solved the problems of their own day. Point, if you will, at their hard-toed boots, thick shorts and shinguards: but who can doubt the ability of Alex James, who learnt the game bare-foot on waste ground, to have played in the lightweight, glove-tight boots of today? How many modern stopper centre-half-backs could blot out Tommy Lawton in the air? Sir Stanley Matthews was active from the inter-war until the 'modern' period, and the up-to-date backs of his old age found no more effective methods of stopping him than those of his youth in the 'ancient' period.

There is no doubt that these players were great. Few would dispute that, if Duncan Edwards were alive today, he would be as pre-eminent at the highest level of football as his contemporary Bobby Charlton, or that he would have been an automatic choice for England's World Cup winning team.

Danny Blanchflower made the transition from the football of Barnsley to that of the World Cup because he was a naturally great player. In any game a man can only meet the challenge of his time and add something to the higher levels of technique. All of these footballers did that.

Conclusively we must say that any team manager who could deploy John Thompson in goal, Willie Woodburn at centre-half-back with Danny Blanchflower and Duncan Edwards as his wing-half-backs, Stanley Matthews on the right wing, Lawton and John Charles as the dual centre-forward prong (what a manager's dream!) with Alex James to serve them from inside-left – would reckon his chances of winning the World Cup a certainty – so long as the other three men could walk.

When all this is said, it must be admitted that footballing memories often are short. No one who saw any of these men is, if pressed, in doubt of their greatness, or their ability to rise to the top of the football of any period. Often, though, the elder among football watchers is at a loss to recall, to an extent convincing to his juniors, the elements of the greatnesses of the heroes of his youth. That is why, in this book, writers who knew and watched these great men have been asked to set down their first-hand memories.

For myself, these names evoke deep memories. As a small boy, I saw Alex James, playing for Preston North End, blast in two of the strongest and most accurate half-volley shots I have ever seen in my life. Two years later, still a schoolboy, I watched his first match for Arsenal – against Leeds United, on a blazing day at

Highbury when I was one of the many in that huge crowd who fainted in the heat.

It is one of my most tragic memories that I saw Duncan Edwards' last match in England – also at Highbury – but it echoes in my mind with his two great Wembley performances against Scotland – in the England sweep of 1955, and when he scored the dramatic late winning goal in 1957.

Perhaps Sir Stanley Matthews and Tommy Lawton spent the years of their greatest power during the second World War but both before it and for long after it they demonstrated a degree of mastery of the ball, the game and their opponents which no one else in those positions has since excelled in any country.

The tragic death of John Thompson chimes in with that of Duncan Edwards: each was deeply mourned by thousands who had never, in the strict social sense, met them: each was, in his own way the symbol of a club; in the case of Edwards, the symbol of a team lost in disaster.

Of John Charles and Danny Blanchflower it is sufficient to say that if they were now in their prime, the record for a transfer fee would be broken tomorrow for either of them.

This is the degree of genius which this book attempts to celebrate and to honour. There is greatness in football in any age: but it is not, I believe – after having watched top class play for almost forty years – an exaggeration to say that these men are great beyond the standards of any particular age.

NOTES ON THE CONTRIBUTORS

Bernard Joy: born 1912: Centre-half for Corinthians, Casuals, Arsenal and England: the last amateur player to win a full cap for England. Author of *Forward Arsenal* and *Play Better Football*: football writer formerly for *The Star* and now for the *The Evening Standard*.

John Rafferty: born 1918: Football, boxing and general sports writer for *The Scotsman* and *The Observer*.

Terence Delaney: born 1913: Author of *A History of the F.A.*, *A Century of Soccer* and, (with Maurice Edelston) *Masters of Soccer*: editor of *The Footballer's Fireside Book*, script writer, B.B.C., sports writer for *The Sunday Times*.

Albert Barham: born 1921, formerly football correspondent of *The News Chronicle*, now of *The Guardian*.

Hugh McIlvanney: born 1934: formerly with *The Scotsman*, now football correspondent of *The Observer*: author of *World Cup, 1966*, chosen 'Sports Writer of the Year' 1966.

H. A. – Tony – Pawson: born 1921: outside-right for Oxford University, Pegasus, Corinthian-Casuals, Charlton Athletic and England (amateur): batsman and outstanding fieldsman for Winchester (captain 1940), Oxford University (captain 1948): football and cricket correspondent for *The Observer*.

Arthur Walmsley: born Lancashire 1917: since 1932 general and sports writer with Kemsley newspapers, *The Sporting Chronicle*, *Daily Dispatch*, *Daily Express*, *Sunday Chronicle*, *Manchester Evening Chronicle*: now northern sports columnist for *The Sun*, long and closely associated with Manchester football.

Brian Glanville: born 1933: formerly free-lance sports journalist in Italy: author of two outstanding volumes of short stories about football – *The Bad Streak* and *The Director's Wife* and several novels, notably *Along the Arno*, *The Bankrupts* and *Diamond*: author of *Soccer Nemesis*, *Soccer Round the Globe* and, with Jerry Weinstein, a *History of The World Cup*: football correspondent of *The Sunday Times*.

CONTENTS

11

ILLUSTRATIONS

ONE

Alex James
by Bernard Joy

ALEX JAMES was not simply a great player. He made other players great. He provided the spark which ignited the genius in the men around him. He gave unity, purpose, drive to a team, and so lifted the entirety. In the four years before James joined Arsenal, dynamic manager Herbert Chapman had converted the club from a struggling, bottom-of-the-table outfit to near-championship class, by reshaping tactics and introducing players of the calibre of David Jack, Tom Parker, Eddie Hapgood and Herbie Roberts. The arrival of James provided the finishing touch. He transformed Arsenal into the kings of world football.

Arsenal had scaled the summit and just completed a championship hat-trick when I joined them as a starry-eyed amateur in 1935. Quite frankly, I hero-worshipped my new colleagues but I do not think my judgment of James was affected. Indeed, for me, he was an aloof figure and I did not appreciate his true value until he retired two years later. The mammoth efforts to replace him and to regroup forces, were a tribute to his greatness. My view of Arsenal's debt to James echoes that of the late Tom Whittaker, who served the club as trainer and manager from 1927 to 1956 while they won all their major honours. 'Alex did more for Arsenal than any other player' he used to say.

James is accepted in Scotland as 'the greatest Scottish inside-forward.' This tribute is from a country where the skilful craft of a midfield general is revered more than flamboyant goal-scorers. The label still does not convey, however, how he set a stamp on Arsenal which was to last nearly thirty years, how he was the torch-bearer of tactics which swept the world and how he helped to make Arsenal the most famous name in football.

Yet he himself had to be transformed first. The crisis came in January 1930, seven months after he had joined Arsenal. In the previous June, Herbert Chapman had beaten Liverpool, Manchester City, Aston Villa and Birmingham to sign him from Preston for £9,000. Chapman needed a midfield player to link defence to attack and there were serious misgivings as to the wisdom of the choice. James was already an established international and had been one of the dazzling stars in the Wembley Wizards, who beat England at Wembley 5–1 the previous year. He was an individualist, a goal-scorer and fond of the limelight. He had said 'The prime duty of

17

the defence is to feed the forwards and I am not going to chase back to get the ball.' Yet this was the man Chapman wanted to drop back as an extra defender in order to make goals for others.

By the turn of the 1929-30 season, the doubts of the pessimists had been confirmed. James had not mastered the positional play expected of him and when he had the ball he held it too long, with the result that his colleagues had been picked up by an opponent by the time he passed the ball. The attack suffered in particular and there was even gloomy talk of relegation. The forward line of Joe Hulme, David Jack, David Halliday, Alex James and Charlie Jones – all internationals – was, at £34,000 in transfer fees, the costliest in football, and a failure.

With the League title out of reach, all attention concentrated on the F.A. Cup, and Arsenal were favoured with a home draw against Chelsea. During the three Christmas matches Chapman brooded over the composition of the team, and particularly the forward line. Finally he decided there was no alternative and took the boldest decision of his career. He dropped James.

The gamble paid and Arsenal beat Chelsea 2–0. Arsenal were in luck too, in the next round, being drawn at home to Birmingham. Chapman fielded the same team, with Len Thompson at inside-left, but this time the formation did not work so successfully. At one stage Arsenal were two up but Birmingham fought back to equalise and forced a replay on the following Wednesday.

The team was in the melting pot again. Once more Chapman acted boldly and this time he coloured his action with dramatic tones to appeal to the showmanship in James. Early on the Sunday morning he drove round to James's home, strode into the bedroom, where James was still in bed, and told him 'Get up Alex. You're coming to Highbury for training because you will be playing in the replay.'

In the train going to Birmingham, James, usually a chatterbox, sat silent and fidgety, realising the crisis, both for the club and himself, immediately ahead. The dramatic recall brought home to him more clearly than any number of heart-to-heart talks, that he had the ability to do the job assigned to him and that the future of the team depended on how well he accepted the responsibility.

Arsenal won 1–0, by a penalty goal. There was nothing sensational or dramatic about the performance of the side, or of James. But the pattern had been established and James had regained the confidence he needed for his vital part. From this point, optimism took over from pessimism, as the club stormed onwards.

Two difficult away ties, against Middlesbrough and West Ham, were surmounted without conceding a goal. Arsenal made heavy weather of the semi-final against Second Division Hull, winning the replay after being two down in the first match, to reach the final for the second time in three years. Their opponents, Huddersfield, the club Herbert Chapman had managed before he joined Arsenal, were strong favourites. They had a brilliant right wing of Alex Jackson, who had been a member with James of the Wembley Wizards, and Bob Kelly, and fielded seven internationals.

Arsenal won 2–0. James gave Arsenal the lead after nineteen minutes, helped heroically in the defence as Huddersfield hit back with cut and thrust football, and made the pass from which Jack Lambert went through to score the second goal near the end. So Arsenal brought home a major honour for the first time and began their long period of ascendancy in British football.

Alex James was born in the mining village of Mossend, near Glasgow, in 1902. His first job was with the local steelworks, where he formed a friendship with Hughie Gallacher, who was also destined to become a Scottish forward of genius and a Wembley Wizard. The pair were known as 'the inseparables,' although they were unlike, Gallacher being a withdrawn, moody, quick-tempered and truculent introvert. They learnt their football together, with a paper ball, tied tight with string, in the narrow streets of the village, as did many of the great players during the period between the two great wars.

James, graduate of the Glasgow junior club Ashfield, was transferred to Raith Rovers and moved to Preston for £3,275 in 1925. There he won four caps for Scotland and the club became known as 'Alex James and ten others.' And so he moved on to Arsenal for £9,000 in 1929 as an established player with a big reputation.

James was only 5 feet 6 inches tall, but he was stockily-built and had very strong legs. He had his hair parted in the middle and plastered firmly down, wore sleeves buttoned at the wrists and had knee-length shorts, flapping and baggy. He had a trademark all of his own, the 'fluttering foot.' With the body shielding the ball from the man tackling him, he would bring a foot, preferably the right, over the ball, pretending to back-heel. The wag of the hips in-variably sent the opponent going the wrong way, while the foot went back over the ball and the instep curled caressingly round it, pulling it back to his bidding. It was a trick which was extensively copied, and never bettered.

His habit of screening the ball from the tackler with his body, earned him innumerable hard knocks on the back of the legs. He was bruised there so often that Tom Whittaker tried to devise 'shinguards' to go on the back of the legs. He took the battering, a lot of it illegal, as part of the price he had to pay for the dominant role in the team, and he rarely lost his temper, or retaliated. So courage must be added to the other footballing virtues, which drew this tribute from George Allison, the successor to Herbert Chapman at Arsenal: 'He is the greatest exponent of all the arts and crafts known to Association Football.'

The baggy pants made James unmistakable on the field. Why did he wear them? Was it showmanship, which demanded he should be the centre of attention? Was it to make him an easy target for passes from colleagues, looking for a man with their head down over the ball? James's own explanation was typical. 'It was to keep my knees warm on a cold day,' he said.

In the same vein was the reason he gave for scoring three goals against Sheffield Wednesday in a League game at Highbury. His reputation as a goal-maker was so established by then that Wednesday manager Billy Walker, a former England inside forward, decided to ignore him as a potential scorer, allow him to hold the ball to his heart's content in midfield, and concentrate on marking the men to whom he could pass. It was similar to the plan Birmingham adopted – without success – in the 1956 Cup Final against Don Revie, Manchester City's withdrawn centre-forward.

James spotted the plan and went through on his own, with an impish grin on his face, to score a hat-trick. So in one match he equalled his total for season 1923-3, when Arsenal amassed 118 goals. He put down this burst of scoring to a question of parental dignity. His 13-year-old son had returned from a schools match that very morning, having scored four goals. 'That's more than you've scored all season' he told his father. As Alex said 'What is a poor father to do,' It was the only hat-trick of his career and he scored only one more goal for Arsenal that season.

His colleagues were less complimentary. In the bath afterwards they said that James would not have scored at all, except for two deflections by defenders and one by an Arsenal man.

It was like James to hide a deep knowledge of the game under a whimsical sense of fun. He was both proud of his craft and humble about his ability. He was self-willed and self-disciplined, a brilliant individualist and a whole-hearted team man, headstrong and amenable.

The perverse blend of his character explains why he surrendered as readily as he did to Herbert Chapman's demand to change from a goal-scorer to a midfield forager. If Chapman is praised for seeing that James was the missing piece in the jig-saw, and then wooing him, silver-tongued, in the same way as he converted Cliff Bastin from an inside-forward to an outside-left and George Male from a wing-half to a right-back, then James also must be congratulated for logically accepting the situation, although part of him was strongly resentful.

Chapman and James were both forceful personalities, firm in their conception of how the game should be played and the team organised, and accustomed to having their own way. So clashes between the two were inevitable.

In May 1931 James refused to re-sign because of a grievance and kept the club on tenterhooks until the following August. As summer wages were automatically stopped in those days, he accepted a post as sports adviser to Selfridges, before finally coming to terms with Arsenal.

Two years later the breach was more serious, when he refused to play in a friendly match in Belfast against Cliftonville in the last week of the season, and was dropped from the final League match. As a result he stayed away from the celebration banquet for winning the First Division Championship and the vice-captain, Charlie Jones, was presented with the Championship cup by John McKenna, President of the Football League. Arsenal took the first step as peace-makers and sent James on a fortnight's holiday to Bournemouth. While he was there he received a telegram from the club saying they had booked him on a sea cruise, starting from Southampton. James accepted with alacrity, expecting a trip through the Mediterranean or to the West Indies, in a luxury liner. When he arrived at the dock, he found it was a grubby cargo boat on a delivery run to Bordeaux. He had to be almost forced on board, but in the end he enjoyed the trip.

In 1925, the year Herbert Chapman joined Arsenal, the offside rule was altered, reducing the number of opponents between an attacker receiving a forward pass, and the goal, from three to two. At this time the full-backs covered the middle, the wing-halves were out wide, taking the wingers, and the centre-half had an attacking role in midfield. Under the old offside rule the game had become stagnant. Using a tactic devised by Bill McCracken of Newcastle, both backs took up position near the half-way line and as soon as an attack developed against them, one would advance, thus throwing the forwards offside.

The whistle was going continuously. It was not unusual to have forty stoppages for offside in a match. Goals were at a premium. Huddersfield won the Championship in 1924-5 with 69 goals, Nottingham Forest scored 29 while being relegated and Manchester United won promotion from the Second Division with as many points as goals – 57. Spectators were losing interest.

Chapman was the first to realise how to capitalise fully on the changes. Sheltered by the offside rule, backs had become slow and cumbersome, and the best device to take advantage was a swift counter-attack. So Chapman plumped for a strong, burly and fast centre-forward as the spearhead through the middle, and raiding wingers to operate in the newly-opened territory behind the wing-halves. Foreseeing how the battering ram centre-forward could play havoc with a defence, Chapman decided to police him with a specialist, converting the centre-half into a stopper or third back. He moved his own backs out to counter the wingers and brought the wing-halves in to take the inside-forwards.

He virtually turned the team formation upside down. He tightened the defence and gave punch to the attack. The vital element in the new tactics was the speed with which an attack on his own goal could be translated into a decisive thrust deep into the enemies' lines. Any delay, and the defence, however slow-moving, would have time to recover.

This is where James was all important. He picked up clearances from the defence and put the front runners away with well-judged passes. He always seemed to be in the space within easy reach when a defender was making a pass. What impressed me most when I came to play behind him, was the way he picked up my misheaders or sliced kicks. Obviously he must have watched closely the way I shaped at the clearance in order to read where the ball was going.

Then, with a shuffle and wag of the hips, he would control the ball and almost immediately speed it on its way. The most spectacular pass was the far-flung one, hit while still facing his own goal, up the right wing to make the fullest use of Joe Hulme's burst of speed. The most fruitful was the through pass for burly Jack Lambert, and later Ted Drake, to shoulder a vivid path through the middle. The most dangerous was the least publicised – the 'killer' inside the right-back for Cliff Bastin. It used to go so near the back that he was lured into thinking he could get it.

In a matter of seconds Arsenal broke away from a desperate defence of their own goal, to have the ball in the back of the other net, with opponents wondering what had hit them. It was twentieth century, terse, exciting, spectacular, economic, devastating. After years of stultifying midfield play, regularly punctuated by the whistle for offside, the spectators loved the electrifying changes and flocked to see Arsenal. But on many an opponent's ground the cry 'Lucky Arsenal' was raised because the visitors snatched both points, often with a comfortable goal margin, after having much less of the game territorially.

A typical move was a header from Herbie Roberts, the first stopper centre-half, a swinging pass by James, and a run by Hulme for Bastin, closing in in anticipation, to score. In one season Bastin had 33 goals, which still stands as a record for a wingman in the First Division, and Hulme had 20. The club's total was 118, to which James contributed three.

The moves themselves were simple enough, but they depended on the supreme skill of James at the focal point. He required anticipation, positional sense, control, stamina, ability to pass accurately, confidence. Once the pattern of moves was known, he had to have tactical sense as well, in order to keep a step ahead of opponents. This, too, he acquired, and an example was the 1930 final. On the coach going to meet Huddersfield at Wembley, he pulled himself out of his seat to tell Bastin 'If we get a free kick in their half, I'll give you a quick pass, slip it straight back and I'll have a crack at goal.'

Some players were not sure whether he was joking, because of his role as a provider of goals, rather than a scorer. But he was deadly serious and when he was brought down halfway in the Huddersfield half, he jumped to his feet, glanced at the referee for permission to go ahead placed the ball and sidefooted it to the left wing without straightening. Bastin cut in, drew the defence, slipped the ball back and James scored.

James was confined almost entirely to a defensive role when Arsenal ran up against a team in top form. Such happened in the semi-final of 1932 against Manchester City at Birmingham. City were a powerful side, with the dangerous left wing of Fred Tilson and Eric Brook given close support by Matt Busby, the genius behind the modern Manchester United. For long periods Arsenal were hemmed in their own penalty box, as City came at them with a virile mixture of skill and power. James was virtually a full-back as Arsenal clung desperately on for a replay. Almost on time, he scrambled the ball away to Bastin, who had been pulled back to the penalty area. Bastin glanced up. There were three light blue shirts and one red – Jack Lambert – on the half-way line. He hit the ball up the right wing and set off in support as Lambert gave chase. Lambert caught the pass just before it crossed the bye-line, centred and Bastin was on his own to score the only goal of the match.

James was assisted in midfield by Charlie Jones in the early days and from 1934 onwards by Jack Crayston, a tall and elegant wing-half bought from Bradford. The other wing-half, first Bob John and then Wilf Copping, a hard-as-nails ex-miner, was mainly a defensive unit, tucking himself close to the third back centre-half. The old-fashioned W-formation attack, with the inside-forwards providing the bases, gave way and Arsenal's other inside-forward, David Jack, was permitted to concentrate on attack.

So the basic formation of the team was virtually 4–2–4, although, of course, numbers were not used in those days. When under pressure Arsenal called back two forwards so that they operated 4–4–2, as modern Manchester United do when they start off in a tough away game, especially in European competition. Herbert Chapman claimed that his motto was 'We want eight men in defence and seven in the attack.' The willingness to drop back to help the defence, and the ability to throw men upfield in a sharp counter-attack, led to his ideas being put into operation.

Arsenal did not have the fluidity which followed the modern advances to the 4–3–3 formation in the last few years, with the ten outfield players being practically interchangeable, overlapping backs becoming wingers, and forwards clearing off their own goal-line, when not switching places across the field. Arsenal of the 1930's were more static and similar to the late 1950's, when 4–2–4 was becoming universally adopted. So, the wingers usually kept to their own touchlines, although both were encouraged to come in to meet the centre when the colleague on the opposite wing had broken away.

The attack when Arsenal won the Cup in 1930 – Joe Hulme, David Jack, Jack Lambert, Alex James and Cliff Bastin – was the best in the club's history. The wingers had the speed and finishing powers to capitalise on the greater freedom wrung out of the change in the offside rule by Arsenal's revolutionary tactics. For Jack, Arsenal paid Bolton the first £10,000 fee – £11,500, in fact – in October 1928. Tall and graceful, Jack dribbled with a high-stepping run as though the ball was attached to his feet, and was an automatic choice for England. A goal he scored against Aston Villa is still talked about at Highbury. He started from the half-way line, left half-a-dozen opponents behind him, half of them sprawling on the ground, and finished the mazy run by dribbling the ball into the goal and turning round with one hand holding the net and a disdainful look on his face, to survey the havoc he had caused.

Arsenal have had more accomplished centre-forwards than Jack Lambert. Ted Drake, who succeeded him in 1934, came nearest to the ideal of an Arsenal leader, with a single-minded devotion in cleaving a path through the middle, irrespective of opponents, or personal injury. Lambert, a former miner and as big-hearted as he was broad-shouldered, was by no means a neat and skilful footballer. Herbert Chapman was always on the hunt for a superior player and imported, at high expense, Scottish international David Halliday from Sunderland, Ernie Coleman from Grimsby and Jimmy Dunne, an Irish international, from Sheffield United in a dramatic signing which was completed shortly before a home match. Each time Lambert was dropped for the new man, and each time he forced himself back into the team. He broke the club's individual scoring record with 38 goals in 1930-1.

Lambert can be classed – with all respect – as an efficient work-man among the artists. But Jack and Bastin will be ranked among the game's immortals and Hulme, of the electrifying burst of speed, won nine England caps. Yet James was the general controlling all four. He lifted the entire attack up to its eminent peak. He held them together and gave them purpose by his magnetic personality and tactical genius.

There have been forward lines in other clubs to compare with Arsenal's of the 1930's: Huddersfield of a few years before – Jackson, Kelly, Brown, Stephenson, Smith; Manchester United just after the war – Delaney, Morris, Rowley, Pearson, Mitten; Spurs of 1962 – Medwin, White, Smith, Greaves, Jones.

Comparison over the decades is impossible, but two facts are certain; the Arsenal forwards made the greatest impact on their contemporaries and they would have been at home in any tactical style, given time to acclimatise themselves to differences in pace, fitness and formation.

In the eight seasons James was at Highbury Arsenal reached the F.A. Cup final three times, winning twice; carried off the League title four times; were runners-up once; narrowly missed the Cup and League double; won the F.A. Charity Shield on four occasions; and set up a First Division points record. In the rest of Arsenal's 82 years history, they won the Cup once, were runners-up twice and won the Championship three times.

On the occasion when Arsenal were the beaten finalists during James's reign – against Newcastle in 1932 – he missed the Wembley match because of injury. The set-back happened on Easter Saturday, when Arsenal met West Ham – then struggling bravely, but in vain against relegation – at Upton Park. The pitch was bare and hard, the lively ball bounced away from James and he collided with 'Big Jim' Barrett, the hefty West Ham centre-half. He damaged the ligaments of a knee and Tom Whittaker was so concerned that he rushed James straight back to Highbury for treatment, arriving there before the match at Upton Park was over.

During the next anxious weeks Whittaker worked night and day to get James fit, making the fullest use of the six-weeks gap between semi-final and Wembley. Ten days before the final James came through a run-out in the reserves and stayed at Highbury for treatment during Cup final week, while his colleagues went to Brighton for their usual seaside toning-up. James joined them on the Friday to have his vital test. All went well. He was able to sprint, kick, turn, dribble and shoot. The players were beginning to leave the field when Whittaker summoned him for the last hurdle – a tackle against himself. Whittaker blocked the ball at

James's feet, put his shoulder to James and with a cry of pain James hobbled away.

For the final Herbert Chapman moved Cliff Bastin to inside-left, switched Bob John from left-half to outside-left and brought in George Male. Although John gave Arsenal the lead, Newcastle won, thanks to the most controversial goal in the history of Wembley finals. Newcastle inside-right Richardson chased a long pass and the ball appeared to be over the line before he centred. Arsenal defenders relaxed as the ball came across, Allen, unmarked for once, headed home and referee W. P. Harper pointed to the middle. Photographs showed that the ball was dead before it was centred, but a goal it was and the initiative was now with Newcastle. Without the ebullient James to restore confidence, Arsenal did not get on top again.

James's injury came at a crucial time in the League as well. They were second, a point behind Everton with a match in hand, when they played West Ham. While ten men held on to a draw at Upton Park, Arsenal did not win another match before the final and Everton increased the lead to six points. After the final, which was then staged on the third Saturday in April, Arsenal took seven points from four games, to cut Everton's lead to two points.

So the club fell between two stools, finishing runners-up in both major competitions. It was the nearest to the Cup and League double this century until Manchester United went into the 1957 final as League champions. Spurs, of course, brought off the fabulous achievement in 1960-61 season.

The magnificent failure followed a season in which the Arsenal machine slid into top gear and everything entered for was won, except the F.A. Cup. They started by winning the opening five matches, the first defeat was in the tenth game and they regained the winning path in the next game by beating Manchester United at Old Trafford for – incredible though it may sound nowadays – United's eleventh successive defeat.

Despite Arsenal's dominance this season, there was an exciting challenge until early spring from Sheffield Wednesday and Aston Villa. The biggest set-back was by 5–1 by Villa at Villa Park, when James was injured. Villa kept up the struggle so well until the last few weeks that the team was invited to the celebration banquet.

Arsenal brought the Championship to the south for the first time. They set up records – 66 points, only 4 defeats and 28 victories.

There was a remarkable similarity between the home and away records, thus showing that they had achieved what many modern teams have failed to do – a style which is equally effective home and away. The records were:

	P	W	L	D	Goals		Pts
Home	21	14	2	5	67	27	33
Away	21	14	2	5	60	32	33

In February they followed a 9–1 home win over Grimsby with a 7–2 away win over Leicester. They totalled 127 goals in the League – 40 more than their previous best.

In the F.A. Cup Arsenal beat Aston Villa, but lost in the next round to Chelsea. In this season the F.A. introduced the idea of putting the Charity Shield up as an annual contest between the Cup holders and League champions. Arsenal beat Sheffield Wednesday and went on to take part in seven of the next nine contests. They won the Sheriff of London Shield, beating famous amateurs Corinthians, the London Challenge Cup, the Football Combination – for the fifth time running – and the Northampton Charity Shield.

Arthur Rowe, manager of the 'push-and-run' Spurs of the 1950's, recalls how his father took him to White Hart Lane as a young boy, to see his schoolboy idol, Huddersfield inside-left Clem Stephenson, for the first time. Rowe was bitterly disappointed. There were no spectacular dribbles, no non-stop runs, no fierce shots. It was not until Rowe's father pointed out that every clearance from the defence seemed to find Stephenson, who immediately switched the ball to a danger point in the attack, that Rowe realised how he was the hub of the entire side, linking defence to attack.

James had a similar role with Arsenal. Admittedly, he was more flamboyant, catching the eye with baggy pants, sleeves rolled down and that curious shuffle over the ball, but the fact remains that the vital part he played in the machine was overlooked. Other clubs were studying Arsenal intently, forced to do so by the stream of successes. The switch of the centre-half to be purely a stopper, stood out like a sore thumb, especially when the man was unmistakable on the field, flame-haired Herbie Roberts. It was easy to spot, too, the bustle, speed and determination needed by the advance forwards. But the subtlety provided by James's strategic ability, his positional sense and passing skill was often overlooked.

So instead of having a general in midfield to harness the forces, imitators were content on getting the ball as quickly as possible from defence to the raiding forwards, bridging the midfield gaps with a hefty kick. So kick-and-rush football was born.

A few clubs, notably West Bromwich Albion, stuck for a time to the old-fashioned formation, with an attacking centre-half, as did some foreign countries, notably Austria and Uruguay, both of whom had outstanding teams before the war. But most English clubs fell over themselves to get on the band wagon of the WM formation, many of them, alas, emphasising the destructive side, but missing the constructive element provided by James, although it was signposted by the heavy number of goals the club were scoring.

Whatever mistakes imitators were making, the hard fact remained that competition was stiffening, especially from the northern clubs, against the London upstarts who had ousted them from their long supremacy. Moves were being recognised, marking was tighter and determination to defeat Arsenal was more intense.

So the Championship hat-trick of 1932-5 ranks as the greatest feat in Arsenal's history and possibly the most sustained period of ascendancy by any club in the Football League. True, Huddersfield also achieved a hat-trick, but it was in 1923-6, when competition soon after the 1914–18 war was much less severe. A factor which made Arsenal's performance even more impressive was the death of Herbert Chapman, the guiding genius, half way through the period, in January, 1934.

The team at the start of the run was: Moss; Parker, Hapgood; Jones, Roberts, John; Hulme, Jack, Lambert, James, Bastin. The average age was nearly thirty. By May 1935, James had to be saved for vital matches, and took longer to recover from injuries, so heavy had been the toll of the close marking he received. Only three of the original eleven, Hapgood, Roberts and Bastin, were regular choices. Parker, Jones, Jack and Lambert had retired, while Moss was fighting a vain battle against a shoulder injury.

Big transfer fees were paid for new men, wing-halves, Jack Crayston and iron man Wilf Copping; Ted Drake, a large-hearted dynamo of a centre-forward; two West countrymen to form a right wing, Ray Bowden and Ralph Birkett; farmer's boy Alf Kirchen and Irish international Jimmy Dunne. Youngsters Les Compton, George Male and Pat Beasley were introduced. And the most intense search of all was to find someone to wear James's mantle, because Chapman feared that the sudden disappearance of a key man could lead to the collapse of the side, as with Spurs without Arthur Grimsdell in the 1930s and Preston without Tom Finney, Wolves without Billy Wright, in post-war football.

It speaks volumes for the generalship of the established players, notably James, Hapgood and Bastin, that the wholesale changes were made so smoothly. The team was literally in the melting pot, being completely rebuilt, and the newcomers had to be guided along the right lines. And yet Arsenal stayed at the top of the First Division for three years while this was going on.

James was badly injured in the opening match of the 1933-4 season against Birmingham at Highbury and was not his real self again until after Christmas. He was out of all four F.A. Cup ties of the season and the sharp drop in the goals-for column to 75 is an indication of how much he was missed. In the next season, full power returned to the attack, with Drake a devastating spearhead, amply supplied with chances by James.

Although not as devastatingly superior as they had been in winning the championship in 1930-1, Arsenal had at least a three-point margin in carrying off the title in each season of the hat-trick. The chief challengers changed each season, first Aston Villa and Sheffield Wednesday, then Huddersfield and Spurs and finally Sunderland and Wednesday again.

It is a pity that Arsenal were not able to pit themselves against European competition during this period. The four British countries kept aloof from any attempt to start foreign competition, at club or international level. They stayed outside F.I.F.A. until 1950 and did not enter the World Cups of 1930, 1934 and 1938, although the door was opened slightly by entering the Olympic Games of 1936.

Standards abroad were rising fast, especially in Central Europe and South America, and would have provided an intriguing yardstick for the new methods and teamwork of Arsenal. There was one important match against a foreign side – in December 1933 against a Vienna XI, which was virtually the Austrian team which had nearly scored the first victory against England on English soil the previous year. The Austrians had drawn with Scotland at Hampden Park a few days before and Arsenal fielded the attack, Hulme, Jack, Coleman, James and Bastin, to win a fine game 4–2.

In 1930 Arsenal began the annual series of matches against Racing Club de Paris in France, a series which were revived for a spell after the war. Arsenal won very comfortably at first and brought ecstatic notices from the French Press. Joe Hulme was called *'Anguille'* – the eel – Cliff Bastin *'feu d'artifice* – firework – and Alex James was given with all-embracing simplicity the name *'Miracle.'*

During the peak period of 1932-5 in the League, Arsenal sank to their lowest depression in the F.A. Cup – defeat by Third Division Walsall. Injuries and illness robbed Arsenal of five regular players and four newcomers were drafted in. The tackling by the Walsall team, especially on James, was grim, and the narrow ground made it harder to find space. Arsenal's 2–0 defeat still ranks as the biggest giant-killing performance in the F.A. Cup.

Although the veterans in the side were jaded and the newcomers were still establishing themselves, Arsenal won the Cup again in 1936. Goal-scoring power declined once more, partly because of James's loss of efficiency in distribution and partly because Ted Drake had to have a cartilage operation in February. Drake started the season brilliantly, scoring seven goals against Aston Villa at Villa Park to set up an individual record for the First Division, which still stands. The decline in finishing in his absence, as Arsenal struggled through the later rounds of the Cup, encouraged the club to take a gamble in the final. Drake was rushed through his recuperating period to have an outing on the Saturday before the final. The opponents were Aston Villa and he scored the only goal of the match to send Villa into the Second Division for the first time in their history.

Sheffield United, then a Second Division club, were the other finalists and outplayed Arsenal in the first half at Wembley. Arsenal began the second half with a kick-off move they had practised. Drake tapped the ball to Bowden, who pushed it diagonally backwards a few yards. James held until the precise moment before chipping the ball into the gap between the centre-half and left-back, where Crayston had raced as soon as Drake kicked-off. Crayston did not score, but the move broke United's confidence, and the grip they had on the game. Drake scored the only goal of the match near the end.

The writing was now clearly on the wall. An adequate replacement for James had to be found. A young Scot, Peter Dougall, was promoted. Although he had incredible ball control, he did not know the right moment to pass in a match. Cliff Bastin was given an extended run at inside-left, without showing the spark of genius which distinguished him on the wing. Another Scot, stocky Bobby Davidson, was signed from St. Johnstone, but he proved to be more suited to be a striking, rather than foraging, forward.

Man for man Arsenal were not inferior to the all-conquering sides of the previous years – apart from James. He played only nineteen games in season 1936-7, before retiring at the end of the season. And for the first time for seven years Arsenal failed to win a major honour. The unifying element of the side had gone. The defenders were just as effective, negatively, but missed James in front of them to make their clearances constructive. The forwards lacked his service and inspiration.

Having failed to groom Bastin and Davidson as the replacement, Arsenal made the mistake of going into the transfer market in a half-hearted way to find the man, signing Leslie Jones, a Welsh international, from Coventry and George Drury from Sheffield Wednesday. Finally, after two years of hesitation, George Allison, who had succeeded Herbert Chapman as manager, took the plunge and paid a record fee of £14,000 for Bryn Jones of Wolves, in 1938.

For the first season Jones was too conscious of the burden of having to follow such a great player, to give of his best, and the war cut across his best footballing years. But he showed signs in a tour of 1939, when the national teams of Sweden, Belgium and Denmark were handsomely beaten, and immediately after the war, that he could be a very adequate deputy.

Alex James may have gone, but the tactical construction, of which he was the keystone, lived vigorously on. By 1937 every British club and many foreign countries, had followed suit in adopting WM, as it was inaccurately called. Forward lines operated in a W formation, with the inside-forwards as the bases, and man-for-man marking by the defence produced an M formation as counter. Arsenal had several refinements which were not always noticed – James roaming more deeply than his fellow inside-forward; a wing-half, notably Wilf Copping, tucking himself alongside the centre-half; and the backs covering the centre-half on a diagonal line instead of shadowing the wingers. The last variation enabled Eddie Hapgood to accomplish many dramatic goal-line clearances.

As far as Arsenal were concerned, the tactics which swept the

ALEX JAMES 'Alex James was not simply a great player. He made other players great. He provided the spark which ignited the genius in the men around him'

JOHN THOMSON with a fellow Celtic player. 'A great player who came to the game a boy and left it still a boy. He had no predecessor, no successor. He was unique'

1930's were good enough for the 1940's and 1950's. They clung to them even though they did not always suit the players available, and while rival clubs knew exactly what to expect.

There was a revival when Arsenal discovered an inside-forward approaching James in style – another little Scot, Jimmy Logie. He was not as strong, could not employ the crossfield pass as readily and was resentful of being expected to emulate the master. But he had a fine positional sense, sure ball control and good timing of the short pass.

The club found other players to fit the 1930 pattern – Joe Mercer as the defensive wing-half and inspiring captain, Archie Macaulay or Alex Forbes as the aggressive wing-half and Ronnie Rooke to fire thunder bolts from centre-forward. So the Championship was won in 1947-8 and, less surely, in 1952-3, and there were two appearances in the F.A. Cup final in between.

It was not until the late 1950's, however, that Arsenal abandoned the practice of putting the players into strait jackets in order to make them conform to methods suitable to men of different qualities in a different era. Only then did the club fall into step in going for versatile, all-purpose footballers, rather than specialists.

If Herbert Chapman had not died suddenly in 1934, there is no doubt that he would have introduced a revitalising change in order to keep in front of his rivals. In fact, he had already discussed it, even when Arsenal's supremacy was still unchallenged. I am equally certain, that Alex James, too, would have taken a drastic change in style in his stride. His grasp of the game was such that he would not merely have fitted into any tactical system. He would have dominated it.

TWO

John Thomson
by John Rafferty

THE SECOND half of a dull Rangers *v*. Celtic match had dragged for five minutes. It was four o'clock in the afternoon of 5th September, 1931 and, in Ibrox Stadium, a situation they describe in Glasgow as 'a draw, nae fitba' was tediously in the making. The most stern of all football rivals were locked in tame stalemate. They had forgotten about winning – they were only concerned with not losing. There was no hint that soon the most tragic football story of all times was to be enacted, that the most popular player on the field was to be so severely injured that he would die that night.

The play was poor response to the hopes of a writer in a Glasgow morning paper, 'The stage is set. Let's hope that there is a grip underfoot and that old King Boreas is blowing his "kisses" elsewhere. The crowd will be there all right, let's hope they are entertained to a clean, sporting contest, keen as mustard and chockful of thrills.' 75,000 were there, but many were bored. Some were irritated, but some did not care, for they were the more committed supporters segregated, as is the custom at Rangers *v*. Celtic matches, on opposite terracings. If the football did not please them they had an alternative in hurling abuse at the opposing faction behind the other goal – and then, at last, a goal was threatened.

Yet another Celtic attack had broken down. They lost possession and the ball broke to the young medical student, 'Doc' Marshall, as he prowled in Rangers' half of the field. He pushed it square to his captain, Davie Meiklejohn, and Rangers broke from defence. Out on the right, the burly winger, Jimmy Fleming, was already galloping and, as the ball was sent in front of him, a typical Rangers wing raid seemed in the making. Peter McGonagle, a fervent Celtic back, raced to challenge but Fleming dodged him and, seeing the thin Celtic defence, sent the ball low up the middle to Sam English a fair, crinkly-haired Irishman, new to the team.

Only a late fitness test had brought Sam English into Rangers' team that day and that was to prove a cruel twist of fate. He gathered the ball smoothly as it came to him, but had he known how that pass was to blight his life, how the consequences of it were to live with him for the remainder of his days, he would have fumbled and let the ball run to whoever would have it. But he had it and he raced straight at goal. Behind that goal were congregated

37

the most violent of Rangers supporters. At last they were interested: a goal seemed inevitable and they erupted into a wild wave of encouragement. A goal now would surely shatter that 'enemy' who had usurped the Scottish Cup the previous season and who, this season, were being hailed as the team of the year.

John Thomson, the lithe young man in a scarlet jersey who kept Celtic's goal, came out to meet the threat. He was balanced and watchful as a cat waiting to pounce on an approaching prey. On came Sam English, clear of chasing defenders, the ball controlled perfectly and then, as he came near the penalty area, it was running ahead of him in position for the shot. It was then John Thomson exploded into action. He dived forward, his body parallel with the ground as the centre-forward's leg drove into the shot. Celt and Ranger clashed and both went down. The ball passed Thomson's right hand post and he had made yet another great save – but he was not to know of it. That was his last save.

Sam English got to his feet and limped to the prone goalkeeper. He looked briefly and waved frantically for assistance. He knew immediately that the young man on the ground was seriously injured and he forgot the pain in his own knee where John Thomson's head had struck it as he saw the blood spurting and staining the turf. The other players crowded round anxiously and one young Rangers player was spoken severely to by Alan Morton when, foolishly, he said that there was not much wrong with the goalkeeper.

Behind the goal Rangers supporters danced with glee and yelled in exhultation like wild tribesmen in a jungle clearing as they looked down on a fallen victim. Here was a situation to suit the basest of instincts. A foe was stricken and it mattered not that it was the one to whom they would have given grudging praise in the shipyards and the engineering shops for sportsmanship and skill had the question been put. On each side in a Rangers *v.* Celtic encounter there is a hate faction and for them it must be victory at all costs and if blood has to be shed, so what – even innocent blood.

David Meiklejohn, one of the greatest Rangers captains of all time, looked grimly towards the disgusting manifestations of joy, then left the group on the field and strode towards them. He was a terrible figure of anger and a hush spread before him. He raised his hands above his head and demanded silence and there was no denying him. The tumult ceased and those who watched knew for the first time that John Thomson was severely wounded. His fiancée in the stand screamed and rushed to the pavilion. His brother hurried to be at his side. Stretcher-bearers carried him to the dressing room, a doctor quickly diagnosed a compressed fracture of the skull and he was removed to the Victoria Infirmary nearby. The game proceeded self-conciously.

He died at 9.25 that night without regaining conciousness and he was just twenty-three years old. His father and mother were at his bedside along with his two brothers. His parents and one brother had been rushed from the little mining village of Cardenden where he lived and had reached his bedside five minutes before the end. There was a terrible sadness in Glasgow that Saturday night. There were tears in many a hard eye that had forgotten how to cry, sobs in throats that had become unused to tenderness. There might have been some odd few who did not laud John Thomson as the greatest goalkeeper of his time but there was none who had not been won by the charm and the integrity of him.

And then was let loose such a torrent of emotionalism as could have clouded any rational assessment of the quality of this phenomenal young man. The news was proclaimed. 'A flashing, dazzling meteor in the sky of atheleticism has departed as suddenly as he came.' He was, 'the bonny lad from Fife.' That last terrible save was 'a flash of that divine fire that burns out all thought of self when danger assails that to which we are committed.' It is all embarrassing stuff when read now, but in the mood of the time it all seemed appropriate. John Thomson in life was such a young man as inspired thoughts of chivalry, in death one searched for appropriate heroic language. He was a knight on the hard field of football, a gentleman from the coal field of Fife who bore none of the ruggedness of the area.

The contradictions in him set him apart from the others in a tough period in a hard game. Football when he played was a punishing game. Players wore heavy boots with steel-inset toe caps. They could be terrible weapons and, of necessity, legs had to be protected with shinguards, cotton wool and bandages. Shoulder charging was allowed and football was indeed a contact sport. Into this violent scene had swept this young man who looked fresh and clean and innocent, and who *was* fresh and clean and innocent, a young man who brought to goalkeeping the grace and elegance which had previously been glorified only in boys' story books. He was born for heroics and for sentimentality.

Life stood still around Glasgow until he was buried and then he was laid to rest like a king. There were thirty thousand mourners at his funeral and they all tried to crush into the little burial ground at Bowhill near his home in Cardenden. Two special trains carried 2,000 mourners from Glasgow and there were two coaches filled with flowers. Twenty thousand others were at Queen Street Station to see the train away and at stations along the way there were reverent crowds standing bareheaded. Many more travelled by coach and car to Fife that day and this at a time when depression hung heavy on the country and, especially in Glasgow, unemployment and want were rife and money was short. Many a one did without his Woodbines to make the sad journey.

Six Celtic players carried the coffin the half mile from the Thomson house to the grave. On the coffin there was a wreath in the form of goal posts along with his international caps. He had played against all the home countries. In Glasgow there was a memorial service and the theme of the sermon was, 'Greater love hath no man than this, that he lay down his life for his friends.'

The circumstances of John Thomson's death were extraordinary and dramatic and they were bound to inspire wild emotionalism but there had to be a great skill to drive it to such extremes. For long there were annual pilgrimages to the grave in Bowhill and only in recent years, as the football followers of Thomson's generation die off, have the visitors to the grave dwindled to a trickle. Those who saw him, now remember his goalkeeping and not the drama of his death and most of them will argue that they have not seen his like since. Old opponents as well as old team mates will declare unequivocally that he was the greatest goalkeeper of all time – and at twenty-three years of age he had not yet reached his best.

Was he truth or legend? Was he a dashing D'Artagnan who lived only in the tales of his deeds? Could it be that such a gentle hero with those smooth features and the full dark hair swept back, typifying speed, could stand up to the punishment that befell goalkeepers in those days? Then they were given no protection other than that due to players in other positions and most teams had a man detailed to harry and hustle them. It was a punishing position in which to play, and John Thomson had not the appearance of a man who could take punishment.

He had been born in Kirkcaldy but soon the family moved to Cardenden in the heart of the coalfield. He was of mining stock but early he had made up his mind that he would never go down the pits, and eventually this was the decision that turned him to professional football. He played first for the village team Bowhill Rovers but signed later for Wellesley Juniors, the principal Junior team of the area. It was from this club that Celtic signed him when he was seventeen years of age.

Steve Callaghan, a cunning old football character who was Celtic's chief scout, brought John Thomson to Parkhead. He signed most of the great players for Willie Maley, the manager who ruled Celtic sternly for over fifty years. He remembers well the day he coaxed the young Fifer to sign a professional form.

Steve Callaghan remembers, 'We needed a goalkeeper at the time and we had been told about one in Fife. It was a long journey to Fife in those days and it had to be a strong recommendation to get me to travel, but the reports on this player were so good that I made the trip. The game started and I had a look at this goalkeeper and he did look the part: but soon I found myself watching the fellow in the other goal and as the game went on I could not take my eyes off him. Before the game was over I was obsessed with him and I had to have him.'

Steve Callaghan went round to see him after the match and quietly invited him to Celtic Park. He had expected no difficulties with this young man, whose name he had never previously heard mentioned, and in those days scouts missed very little. He was shocked to find the boy reluctant to do business and the reason emerged in a strange story. His mother had dreamed that he had been badly injured playing in goal and had been impressed by the dream and told him of it. Young Thomson knew that his mother would never approve of him signing a professional form – so, too, did Steve Callaghan.

And yet he had to have him, for he knew that this was a very special goalkeeper. He says now 'I knew that if I allowed him to go home I would never get his signature.' There was a long session of persuasive talk before the young man was won over and, when his resistance was broken down, Steve Callaghan held the form against a lamp post for him to sign it and in such unlikely surroundings a great football story began.

A young raw lad from Fife came to Celtic, and to Glasgow, and the club found him digs in the Gallowgate amongst team mates, and with startling suddenness he was to conquer the city, for his success was immediate and total. The club wisely gave him time to become used to the throb of the city: he was loaned to Ayr United for three games to break him in and then he was in the team against Dundee in a League Championship match. He was just turned eighteen years of age.

Those who played with him that day remember his confidence. He did make one mistake that cost a goal. Later in the team bus, as the party journeyed back to Glasgow Mr Tom Colgan, a formidable director, spoke to the young player. 'You did quite well, young fellow,' he said, 'but you had better not lose too many goals like that one today.' Thomson answered innocently, 'Don't worry, sir, that won't happen next week.' He had already picked himself to play in a Scottish Cup tie the following Saturday against the same club. He did play, and played well, and he was established as Celtic's goalkeeper and accepted in all Scotland as a bright new star.

Before John Thomson played in that Cup tie against Dundee, the experienced, hardened men of Celtic were to be shaken by signs that they had among them an extraordinary young man, one who, on the surface, was a raw country laddie, but one who was gifted with such a sharp eye, such co-ordination and athleticism as made him a natural at all ball games. He had taken to goalkeeping for it was the art that gave scope for all his wonderful gifts.

All this had not been readily apparent. The players had been misled by his broad Fife accent and the startled innocence of him when he was confronted with the complexities of city life. He seemed too raw to be thrown into professional football. His early guide in football matters was Jimmy McGrory, that supreme goal scorer who was the idol of all the Celtic faithful. McGrory was moved to look after the young man and he tells just how country style was the new goalkeeper.

He tells how his life was the life of the mining village although, all along, he was determined that he would never go down the pits: but he neither knew nor cared about what went on outside his own little world. Jimmy McGrory remembers Celtic having arranged a game in Dublin and the players looking forward to it as a holiday jaunt and John Thomson being puzzled by the enthusiasm. He knew that there was such a place as Ireland but he seemed to think that civilisation had passed it by. In his broad Fife accent he asked Jimmy McGrory, 'What kind of place is Dublin? Has it got houses like here?'

That was the naïve, callow youth who went for special training with Celtic to the Hydro at Seamill on the Ayrshire coast. Celtic then, as they still do, went there before the start of the Scottish Cup ties and, on the sands and the golf course, got set up for the stern football of the Cup. It was a time of relaxation. Other games and activities took the place of football and eased the tension built up in the early matches of the season. The hotel life, the diversity of sporting activities were all new to the lad from Fife.

John Thomson could have been repressed by the new way of life but as Jimmy McGrory took him by the hand he was to startle his club mates with the athletic gifts he laid before them with the innocence of a young doe. After the first morning's training Jimmy McGrory told him, 'We'll go to the pool now and splash about.' Thomson answered, 'I can't go in there, I can't swim.' Jimmy McGrory told him, 'Don't let that worry you. I can't swim either.' He coaxed him down to the pool where the other players were capering noisily. The young goalkeeper was facing a new experience and was obviously bewildered.

A player dived into the water and Jimmy McGrory told his charge, 'Just throw yourself in like him and that gets the shock of the cold water over quickly. When you get in I'll be beside you and you'll be all right.' He tells of how the young man poised on the edge of the pool and then hit the water in as graceful a dive as he had ever seen and glided under water to the other side of the pool. He had natural grace of movement.

That afternoon the schedule called for golf. Mr Maley, the Celtic manager, was keen on the game as a healthy recreation for the players and what that great and forceful manager liked, all his players *had* to like. John Thomson complained to his guardian Jimmy McGrory that he had never played the game and knew nothing about it. Jimmy McGrory told him what the boss thought about it and that he had better start learning. And so the young fellow went to the course with the other players and Jimmy McGrory, the old hand, got him kitted out and led him to the first tee.

The first hole at West Kilbride, adjoining the Seamill Hydro, has out of bounds on the right and rough on the left and the green is over close to the left rough. It is not altogether straightforward. Jimmy McGrory told his young apprentice not to be ambitious but to knock the ball up the fairway and when they were out of sight of the club house they would see about adding a bit of technique to the play. There is still amazement in Jimmy McGrory's voice when he tells: 'John Thomson took the driver I handed him. He gripped it reasonably well without being told how and then with a swing that any of us would have been proud of he hit the ball far and straight up the fairway. It was the first time that he had had a golf club in his hands.' He had astonishing co-ordination of hand and eye.

That night there was a snooker tournament. Hugh Hilley, the left-back, takes up the tale with some authority. He was the club snooker champion. In his capacity as champion it was his lot to introduce the young man to the game, after he had admitted that he had never been near a billiards table and did not know whether you hit the ball with the fat end or the thin end of the cue. The colours of the balls confused him but Hugh Hilley took him in hand, for it was a rule that the whole party took part in the activities. Celtic were a team even when relaxing. He gave him some elementary instruction, gave him a handicap and he was a competitor.

By this time there was a bit of interest in the young man and a fair crowd to see how he would tackle this new medium for his skill. They were not surprised when the young phenomenon began to pot balls all around the table and won the tournament off a handicap that was aimed at having him eliminated in the first round and out of the way of the serious players. He had a wonderful eye. It was the same story when he came to play badminton. In next to no time he was a better than average player.

Jimmy McGrory, who knew him as well as anyone, says, 'I'm often asked what made John Thomson great. I tell everyone that he was not just a goalkeeper, he was a great natural athlete. He was not big but he had a magnificently developed body with all the grace and litheness of an Olympic gymnast. He had not big hands but he had neat hands and I have never seen hands that were safer in clutching a ball.' There are many stories of the extraordinary power of these hands.

In one game at Hampden Park, they held the ball in what must have been one of the most remarkable saves of all time. The details have been amply verified by those who took part in the match. Celtic were playing Queen's Park, the great amateur club, then a power in the First Division of the Scottish League. Celtic were being hard pressed and conceded a penalty kick. Bob Gillespie, the captain of Queens and the last amateur to captain Scotland, did not shirk his responsibility and pass the kick on to some unfortunate. The Celtic match was the big match of Queen's season for the strange reason that there was a firm friendship between the clubs and it was thus as combative as a fight between brothers.

Bob Gillespie, a great player and a hard shot, took the kick and hit it true and was satisfied that he was scoring and then John Thomson flashed into his dive and not only got to the ball but held it with his arms fully extended. But that was not the strange part of the action. He held the ball not with his hands behind it but with one hand on the top and the other hand beneath, plucking it out of the air. Jimmy McGrory still marvels at that save and Hutton Bremner, who played for Queen's Park that day, goes into ecstasies over it and adds forcibly, 'Anyone who says that there was a greater goalkeeper than John Thomson does not know what he is talking about.'

There was another instance of this special skill in clutching in a game against the English League at Tottenham in 1931. John Thomson lost seven goals that day, but his goalkeeping was generally reckoned the best that had ever been seen. The goal that day was a concert platform for him and on it he received modestly the adulation due the virtuoso. The performance was climaxed by a flourish that did not matter except to show his abundant talent.

The English centre-forward burst through after a running pass but not before the referee had whistled offside. He was furious with frustration and, as John Thomson came out to retrieve the ball for the free kick the centre forward lashed at it. Straight at the goalkeeper it flew rising over his head but he, without breaking his leisurely walking stride, reached up, held the ball and continued his walk and placed it for the free kick. The nonchalance of the action did not hide the skill of the clutch and the cheering and applause must have been the greatest ever for a non-save.

John Thomson, on training days, experimented with various aspects of his trade and at times he would playfully show the power of clutching in his elegant hands. With one finger of each hand he would hold a moderately hit shot, but clutching was but one facet of his perfection. Above all other goalkeepers he had the muscular power to give him agility in mid-air and even to change direction and it was this power that enabled him to make the save that those who played with him rate the best save that he ever made. They voted it the save that no other goalkeeper could have made.

The match was at Celtic Park against Kilmarnock. At centre-forward for Kilmarnock was a legendary character, 'Peerie' Cunningham, whose shooting on the turn gave him his nickname and a reputation for being one of the most dangerous shots in Britain. Peerie pivoted on one pass and lashed at the ball and it seemed to be going for Thomson's right-hand post and he dived in that direction. Too late, it seemed, he saw he had misjudged and the ball was going the other way. With some weird play of his muscles, he twisted in mid-air, turned back the other way and got enough of his fingers to the ball to turn it away from the goal. Attackers and defenders stood dumbfounded in involuntary tribute to the save.

There was another well-remembered occasion in an inter-League match against the English League when he stopped the action with a ridiculous save. It was in 1928 at Birmingham, and the Scots were badly outplayed and yet lost by only 2–1. Throughout it seemed that only John Thomson stood between the English League side and the complete humiliation of the Scots. On one occasion he was on his knees to save a point blank drive and the ball spun to Hine the Leicester City inside-forward who stood unmarked twenty yards from the goal line. Here was the perfect situation for him, for his forté was the powerful, thumping shot, hit deliberately. It was the shot that great inside-forwards of the day had time to unleash, for the marking then was not so tight or the tackling so fiercely fast.

Ernie Hine hit the shot full on his instep and John Thomson was still on his knees as the ball streaked towards the goal, directed to slip under the crossbar and lodge in the roof of the net. And then with a great gymnast's leap John Thomson rose and in a blur of action his body arched and his arms stretched and fingers reached the ball and its path was bent and it rose to clear the crossbar. It was for such saves as this that it was written of him, 'He had the spring of a jaguar and the effortless grace of a skimming swallow.'

There are goalkeepers who are spectacularly efficient at church fairs saving sixpence-a-try penalty kicks, and others who are brilliant when the opposition is ordinary and the stakes are moderate, but the great goalkeeper must produce his best on the big occasion and the more there is at stake the more he must climb to sublime heights. In the memorable matches there is very little between the teams and error can decide a match. Others may slip and escape the full punishment but there is nobody to cover for the goalkeeper and he alone on a football field is allowed no mistake. The responsibility for him on the grand occasion is not only to raise his game but to avoid even one foolishness and ninety minutes is a long time to face under such demands.

The most important match that John Thomson played in was the Scotland v England game at Hampden Park in March 1931. It was a match that had been preceded by much bitterness when the Football League invoked a rule debarring their clubs releasing players for internationals on the day that they had a League fixture, except for their own association. Scotland were not allowed to choose for the match their nationals playing in England, and they had come to depend heavily on them. Scotland, since Anglo-Scots first played in 1896, had only once before played an all home team, the Tartan Eleven of 1925, which beat England 2–0. It was a match of extraordinary tension and the young goalkeeper was to influence the result enormously with one typical athletic save.

The team was in fact a Scottish League team, and such a team had been beaten 7–3 just a few weeks previously at Tottenham. John Thomson, on his goalkeeping that day, was chosen to displace Jack Harkness of the Wembley Wizards but he was about the only one to go into the selection without heavy criticism. Carlton Place, in Glasgow, where the Scotland selectors met to choose their team, was blocked to traffic at times as a crowd gathered to hear the announcement. When it did come there was a heavy silence before the burst of criticism. The most charitable jibe was that it was a team of panic.

Sandy Archibald, who had joined Rangers in 1917 and had last been capped in 1924, seven years previously, was the astonishing outside-right. George Stevenson, who had never played on the right was inside-right. Jimmy Miller of St. Mirren was new to international football and Colin McNab of Dundee had only shown form in club football and had flopped when the class had been raised. Displeasure at the Scotland team did not keep the crowd away from Hampden and when the Prime Minister, Ramsey

McDonald, took his seat, there were 129,810 spectators in the ground and that was, at that time, a record for any sporting event in the world. It was a trying occasion for a young man such as John Thomson, to be the last line of defence in a team that had been pitied and despised, and before such a huge crowd.

When the Scots won the toss, the common joke was that was all they could win, but when half-time was reached, and the goal-keepers had not been beaten there were faint manifestations of Scottish confidence. There was an exciting burst of attacking play from Scotland at the start of the second half such as nobody thought this team capable of, and then, within two minutes, first the elegant George Stevenson, and then Jimmy McGrory, scored and England were two down, but not prepared to accept the position: and they stormed into furious attack.

At the height of it the big South African, Gordon Hodgson, who played for Liverpool, had the goal exposed and hit a mighty shot. John Thomson went for it but the ball struck Meiklejohn and was deflected. The goalkeeper, in mid-air, stretched the extra distance and got one hand to it and sent it past the post. It was a save that took the fire out of the England side, a save that screamed at them that this was not to be their day. Scotland held their two goals lead until the end and then Mr C. F. Sutcliffe of the Football League said 'I'm surprised that Scotland should go to England for players. There's no need for it.' How different might have been the tale had John Thomson not reached Gordon Hodgson's shot.

No other in the unpoetical world of football inspired such rhap-sodies as this athletic young man from the Fife coalfields. It was written of him, 'To see him Saturday after Saturday moving lithely between his posts gave to the fortunate onlookers the same intensity of satisfaction that plays and operas and the high vibrant pitch of great verse convey to minds more interested in things of the spirit.' These are words that could only have come from an educated mind and they must therefore be taken seriously, but they are strange sentiments to have been inspired in those desperate years when hunger and unemployment were embittering Clydeside and red political doctrines were more popular than poetry.

There had to be more to John Thomson than athleticism and agility, a fast eye and easy co-ordination. Goalkeeping such as his springs from an inherent skill, but this has to be polished in practice until it becomes an art: but still that is not enough. He who would be a great goalkeeper must have courage enough to express his art in the hectic goal area where the threat of painful injury is ever present for the one who would push his talents to the limit.

John Thomson's courage was amply evident in his philosophy of goalkeeping as pertaining to that greatest of all threats, the cross ball. Some have been brave and told their defence mates that all cross balls in the goal area, six yards out, are theirs. John Thomson insisted that everything out to the penalty spot, twelve yards away, was his. He argued that he could outjump any forward and that his arms gave him an added advantage and, in effect, he did take everything out to the penalty spot.

He who would wonder where courage comes into this should understand that goalkeepers were treated so much more roughly in these days and that, when they came out from their line, they were fair game for heavy-booted forwards, and the further they came out the greater was the risk to their limbs. John Thomson insisted on going further than the others. He knew how other goal-keepers looked on this matter, for he was a friend of every other one in the League, and his first call when he arrived for a Saturday match was on his counterpart in the opposition and the talk was always of goalkeeping.

The dive at the feet of Sam English which brought death to him was described as courageous and, although some might rate such a description emotional, it was indeed courageous, for it was not a dive into the unknown but one made deliberately by one who had experience of the consequences. The previous February against Airdrie at Celtic Park, he had made such another dive to save his goal and had been carried from the field with a broken shoulder and a shattered jaw. Most goalkeepers would have played it cleverly so soon after such an experience. Maybe, in the instant before he dived, he remembered that other occasion.

John Thomson was established as the Scotland goalkeeper when he died, and that is remarkable for then it took much longer to break through because there were fewer internationals and, indeed, to all intents just those between the Home Countries. Yet by the time he was twenty-three he had been honoured eight times and this was fast progress indeed for a goalkeeper. He was judged to be supreme and, with some awe, it was said that he was still not at his best. Those who argue now that he was the best ever can do

D

so without embarrassment for, although it is ridiculous to compare the old with the new in other positions because of the changing conditions it is relevant to compare goalkeepers. The art is the same now as then.

It should not be thought however that he did not make mistakes. Old Steve Callaghan who discovered him remembers him losing a goal at Firhill which cost Celtic the League Championship. He had the ball in his hands and allowed it to drop over his shoulder. 'He was posing for the cameras,' says Steve.

Those who do not think that a goalkeeper would think of the cameras should hear old Jimmie Brownlie, a great goalkeeping character, tell of the bitterly cold day when he was keeping goal and getting so little to do that he passed the time talking to a young press photographer behind the goal. Later, moved to pity for the shivering youth, he told him, 'The next time the ball comes up here I'll make it look good and you have your camera ready and you'll get a good picture and you can get away home then.' The ball did come up and Jimmy went for it spectacularly in the classic pose but as he tried to hold the position he dropped the ball and it trickled over the line!

There was another occasion when the skill of John Thomson did not break through and left a great public disappointed. Celtic toured America in 1929 and the news of the young goalkeeper extraordinary had gone before them. Everybody, it seemed, wanted to see him in action. The matches were played mostly on baseball pitches and in the heat of summer the grounds were uneven and baked hard. The cantrips of the ball were unpredictable and John Thomson was never able to work out what it was going to do. Not once on the tour did he satisfy. He was a disappointed young man for he had read the pre-match notices and he would not have been human had he not wanted to live up to them.

He was human in another way in that, although he loved football, he saw beyond it and recognised it as no more than a fleeting spell in a man's life. He had begun to prepare himself for the future and worked in a gents' outfitters in the centre of Glasgow. He saw his eventual future as a provider of men's clothing: it was a strange choice from one with his hard Fife background.

There was, however, a soft refined side to his nature and nothing distressed him more than the wicked religious bigotry that muddied the rivalry between Celtic and Rangers. Celtic, the club with Irish origins attracted Catholics although their players were not all of that religion, John Thomson was a Protestant and a member of the Church of Christ in Cardenden. Rangers were exclusively non-Catholic and in the period when he played. the bigotry had shown itself violently on the field and on the terracings.

On the morning of his death Alan Breck, the most influential sports journalist in Scotland at the time, wrote: 'Right away I would express the hope that this season's encounters between the "big two" will be more pleasant affairs than last term. Then, you will remember, rivalry exceeded bounds. Let's hope that the players for their own sakes and for the prestige of the clubs, whose colours they wear, will not forget to be sportsmen first and all the time.' The following week a panel of experts met and admitted that a Rangers *v.* Celtic match represented bad football but that on that awful Saturday although there had been one or two objectionable incidents, the conduct of the players had been no worse than childish.

The gentle nature of the young goalkeeper was hurt by the wild manifestations of hate that came from both sides. Like many another he could not see where religion should influence sport and indeed how religion could be equated with intolerance and hate. Unfortunately the intolerance and hate still persist but is mainly manifest on the terracings and the players behave more rationally than in John Thomson's days.

Then players were apt to hurl religion-tinged insults at one another during a game and the classic story of this, which has often been connected with another, in fact had its origin in John Thomson. At half-time he was sitting very quietly and obviously disturbed. Jimmy McGrory noticed this and asked him what was troubling him. After some coaxing he said, 'That centre has been calling me a papish bastard.' McGrory shook him by the shoulders and told him, 'Don't let that worry you, I get called that every week.' 'That's all right for you,' answered Thomson, 'you are one.'

There was no bitterness or meanness in him and Sam English later told how, near half-time in that last match, when he lunged at a cross from the wing and just failed to get his head to the ball, John Thomson called to him, 'Hard lines, young fellow.' His was the purity of purpose that in a dark age transcended all the bitterness and nastiness that was near him. In a few more minutes he was fatally injured in that dreadful accidental clash with that same young fellow.

Someone at the time wrote, 'A life for a goal – what an unkind and hopelessly unfair exchange.' It was a disturbing thought and there must always be such thoughts when there is death in the sports arena.

A village rhymester wrote his humble farewell:

> 'The unerring eye, the master touch,
> More buoyant than the ball;
> The fearless heart, the powerful clutch,
> The genius, praise them all.

> 'The squirrel's leap, the falcon's flight,
> The clear quick thinking brain;
> All these were yours for our delight,
> Never, alas! again.'

These are happier words with which to remember a great player who came to the game a boy and left it still a boy. He had no predecessor, no successor. He was unique.

THREE

Tommy Lawton
by Terence Delaney

Part of it perhaps is nostalgia. The players we admired long ago have grown taller in our memory, and what they did is gilded and improved by our affection for our own youth. Yet even now, when I see a high centre fly across the goalmouth, the attackers and defenders jostling, their faces turned anxiously upward, I find myself thinking 'If only Lawton was there.'

For me that was one of the unforgettable sights – Lawton, with his smooth and certain stride, moving swiftly and watchfully into position, his dark head jutting forward, and then, at precisely the right moment, gathering himself and rising from his toes in a slow and easy leap, clear above the rest; pausing, it seemed, at the top, and suddenly, with a powerful swinging twist of the neck, striking the ball downwards, right off the centre of the forehead, hard into the goal. Or Lawton, his feet wide apart, lounging and prowling, deceptively relaxed, just outside the penalty area, until the man with the ball let it run just a shade too far; then a pounce, two more strides, and the shot – that incomparable shot, lazily executed apparently, but travelling like a shell, just inside the post, just under the bar. Nothing to be done; the goalkeeper and the backs, still flatfooted, staring at each other with wide-palmed gestures of anger and reproach. Another Lawton goal; in his twenty years of first-class football he scored 500 of them.

The mere presence of Lawton made the best and coolest of defences uneasy. He was skilful, powerful and dangerous, and one of the great pleasures of watching him was that he looked the part. The footballer's strip of the forties – heavy boots, bulging shinpads, big flapping shorts – already begins to look as old-fashioned as the whiskers of Dr W. G. Grace; but even in this gear, at a glance, here was a man born and built to be a footballer. He was six foot tall, and just under thirteen stone. His black hair was slicked back from a widow's peak, each side of straight centre parting. His forehead was broad, with high temples, his face long and intent. His eyes were dark and sharp, and his nose commanding. He was wide enough in the shoulders, and big enough in the chest, but it was the solid muscular power of his neck and legs that were most characteristic of him, conditioned his style, and made him the greatest of all headers of the ball. Powerful as he was, his actions were balanced and graceful. 'He was the lightest mover,' Alex James said, 'of any big man who ever played football.'

55

At the peak of his career, Lawton's reputation in this country, and in any country where football was played, was something extraordinary. Admiration, criticism and controversy followed him everywhere, for he was not only a great player; he carried about with him that extra quality, indefinable but instantly recognisable – he was a star. You felt it the moment he came on the field. You must have felt it even if you knew nothing of his reputation – though in the forties and fifties that was unlikely, unless you were a hermit, or a member of some obscure religious order. Yet the tribute the crowds paid to Lawton was not, on the whole, a tribute of affection. His entrance was greeted, not with that heartfelt roar, and swell of clapping, that meets those who are called the darlings of the crowd. The sound that indicated to the ignorant stranger that this one – number nine – was Tom Lawton was rather a murmur of admiration, and the sibilant noise of some hundreds of the knowledgeable whispering to their neighbours 'That's him.' The roars came later, forced from their chests by the sheer pressure of excitement. This reaction was understandable, for Lawton gave none of his time to gestures of crowd-pleasing, or to those pieces of acting that invite the audience to share the player's feelings.

His manner, waiting for the kick-off, was preoccupied, professional, self-assured. I see him with his arms folded, his shoulders hunched against the cold, tapping his toes into his boots, testing the turf. If the ball came to him, without unfolding his arms, he would swing his shoulders and let his powerful leg follow the movement indolently, a thoughtful picture of force restrained. With the same action, the ball might slide to a team-mate a few paces away, or sail thirty yards to give the goalkeeper a stinging high catch under the bar. His other characteristic attitude, in these minutes before the first whistle went and he glided into action, was a solid stance, feet wide apart, hands on hips, his head thrust forward. Though he ignored the crowd, his expression was not disagreeable, merely neutral. As the teams took their positions, he might recognise an opponent with a sideways nod, or, unexpectedly, you would see his white teeth shine in the most pleasant and relaxed of smiles.

They used to say of the famous Stephen Bloomer, the great goal-scorer of the turn of the century, that he was a 'destroying angel', and the attitude of the crowd to him, it is reported, was much the same as to Lawton. From such players crowds expect goals – with a certain grimness. When the goals do not come, they can turn against them. High anticipation changes quickly to disappointment, then to unreasonable hostility. Lawton himself knew a good deal about crowds, their fickleness and their irrelevance. Billy Wright, later to win a hundred caps and captain England, learned an early lesson from him on the subject. It was Wright's first international, and he was picked, oddly, at inside-left. Lawton nursed and encouraged him, but he had a bad game. The first time young Billy got the ball, he made such a conspicuous mess of controlling it that the crowd laughed. He remembers Lawton's comment – the voice of experience: 'Don't take any notice of those – you'll get a lot of that.'

All this, so far, is the mature Lawton, the player of weight and authority, already arrived at the top of his profession. Even the greatest of footballers, however, begin as little boys kicking a ball about, and, watching them in the park, picking out the unmistakable one to whom this game is a natural and stylish physical expression, one always wonders romantically 'Is this the one – or will he just play with the idea, along with others, skip the hard work, and make his living in some other profession?' Lawton was one of those few who are successful footballers right from the start – Duncan Edwards was another – and there is no evidence that he ever wanted to be anything else. He was born in Bolton, on October 6th, 1919, played for Folds Road Central School and, by the time he was fourteen, was already a notable junior footballer. Even then, his speciality was goals. In three seasons of schoolboy football, he scored the astonishing total of 570. Professional spotters, and a manager or two, travelled considerable distances to see him. The club that signed him was Burnley, then in the Second Division, and he was only sixteen when he played for them in a League match against Doncaster Rovers. Evidently it was a good enough first appearance, because he was picked again the following week against Swansea Town. He scored twice. One was a header, and when it went in there must have been quite a few men in the crowd who nudged their neighbours and remarked that the lad would go far, – without any idea at all of how right they were.

Lawton had to wait until his seventeenth birthday before he could be signed as a professional. He was, promptly, and only four days after that birthday he made his first professional appearance, at centre-forward against Tottenham Hotspur. If ever there was a dream start to a career, this was it. Lawton at this time was leaner, lithe and elastic in his movements, bursting with enthusiasm and ambition. If he had any private anxieties before the game, if any doubt weakened the unusual self-confidence that was always so much a part of him, all that was soon resolved. Only two minutes from the start Brocklebank drove a long pass straight down the middle and young Tom was after it as if he had heard a starter's pistol. He was between the backs at top speed before they had time to close on him, and in full stride hit the ball with all his force. This was the first public appearance of the authentic Lawton cannon-ball and, before or since, there have been few sights in football to equal it for excitement. A few minutes later he scored his second, again prophetically typical – a header from a fast out-swinging corner, exactly met at the top of a perfectly judged jump. At his age, and with a hat-trick in sight, coolness was too much to expect and, by his own account, he was in such a state of excitement that he missed two easy open goals before half-time. By the second half he had cooled down, and, offered another chance, he took it calmly.

Lawton, the footballer, was too good for Burnley to be able to keep him. Before he was eighteen he had been transferred to Everton.

Up to this time, incidentally, Lawton, being a natural ball-player, and having some time on his hands in the summer, had been making a local reputation for himself as a cricketer. In 1936 he was in Burnley's Lancashire League side. The professional at that time was the West Indian fast bowler Manny Martindale, and it was just as well that Lawton had the wisdom of such a wily old hand behind him when, at the age of sixteen, in Burnley's match against Nelson, he had to face an even more intimidating West Indian – Learie Constantine. Martindale put in hours at the nets bowling to Lawton, imitating Constantine's style, teaching him how to recognise Learie's deceptive and destructive slower ball. When Tommy went out to bat in the match, the slower ball was the first one Constantine offered him, and he hit it into the football ground for six. The second was the fast one, and, rather to his own surprise, he hit that for six as well. That was the end of the fireworks, but he ended the innings 30 not out. Lawton still has one souvenir of his brief and lively cricket career – and of another six. This one was off the last ball of the last over against Enfield, the bowler was the slow left-hander Jim Bailey of Hampshire and it was the winning hit. They found the ball, and presented it to Lawton at the next annual meeting.

The fee Everton paid for Lawton – £6,500 – was a surprisingly high one for the 1930's, and for a boy of his age. He was worth it. He stayed with Everton for nine years, the years that completed his education as a player, and established him as an international. For the education, Lawton gave most of the credit to the man whose place he was to take as the finest centre-forward and the best header of the ball in the world – Dixie Dean. Dean, the only man ever to score sixty goals in a single English League season, was, like Lawton, born with the ability to flick a heavy ball off his forehead with force, accuracy and style. He taught Lawton how to develop this gift by constant practice, and he taught him, too, that a centre-forward is not simply a human firing-machine, who sees the rest of the forward-line as a toiling gun-crew whose duty is to feed him with scoring chances. Dean saw himself as the leader and organiser of the line, the point on which it swung, the man best placed to change the direction of attack from wing to wing, to draw defences this or that side of the middle, to place opportunities in the gaps he had contrived. Many years later Lawton was using, with destructive effect, one particular trick he had learned from Dean. As a high pass came to him down the middle, Lawton, with his back to the centre-half, would spring sideways to meet it, taking his man with him. Then, quickly, instead of aiming for the goal, he would rap the ball down in the opposite direction to his leap, in a short headed pass to be picked up by his inside-forward coming through. In the early thirties, Dean was making scoring chances like this for Dunn. In 1947, Lawton, with Notts County, was making them for Sewell. So, in such transient physical arts as sport, the history of a game is illustrated and preserved.

Lawton's first two seasons with Everton were good years for him. In 1938 he was top goal-scorer in the First Division – 28 goals – and was given his first England cap. In 1939 he was top scorer again, with 35 goals and won a League Championship medal.

There are certain trophies a footballer likes to have with him when he retires, to keep him company and to encourage a proper sense of respect in the younger generation. Some tuck them away in drawers, but will produce them if asked. Other, simpler, men make an altar of the front-room sideboard, with the medals, plaques, cups and figurines displayed as sacramental plate, or hang the caps and flags on the wall like scalps on the teepee-pole of an ageing Red Indian chief. Of this loot, three specimens are the most highly prized – an international cap, the League medal, and the F.A. Cup-winners' medal. By the time he was twenty, Lawton had collected two of them. The other, in all his years of football, escaped him – he never played in an F.A. Cup Final. It is an odd thing that this last, which depends so much more than the others on luck, has the highest sentimental value. Lawton himself, early in his playing career, listed the Cup medal as one of his great ambitions, along with captaining England – which he did, against France in 1945 – and leading the England forward line against Scotland, which became almost a habit. He played against Scotland for the first time in 1939, at Hampden. England had not won there for twelve years, but they did that time, and it was Lawton who scored the winning goal – headed in, from a perfect Matthews centre, seventy seconds from the end.

His first international was against Wales, at Ninian Park in Cardiff – apart from Hampden the most emotional of international settings for a debut. He was in Burnley on the Wednesday the team was picked, and learned of his selection by ringing up the local evening paper – anonymously. A sub in the sports department read the team over to him. Lawton misheard the name of the centre-forward and asked him to repeat it. 'Lawton, you daft loon!' the man shouted – 'Our Tom!' Wales won the game 4–2, and the Welsh centre-half, Tom Jones, also of Everton, kept his young club-mate pretty well in hand. Lawton did score, however, from a penalty in the second half, and apparently satisfied the selectors watching the game, because immediately after it they picked him to represent England, four days later at Highbury, against the Rest of Europe. This was a commemoration game, arranged to mark the 75th anniversary of the Football Association, but one could hardly have called it either complimentary or friendly. The visitors, representing six European countries, played it rough, and their tactics of obstruction and body-checking, less familiar then than now, enraged the crowd. It is worth mentioning, in case anyone thinks all the grosser incivilities of the game were invented in the 1960s, that the Italian centre-half, Andreolo, spat at the referee. With the directors' box full of Distinguished Persons and representatives of the F.A. and F.I.F.A., Mr Jewell decided to let it go. England won the match 3–0 – one to Lawton.

From his first appearance for England in 1938 to the outbreak of war in 1939, there were eight international matches. Lawton played in all of them, and scored in five. Compared to the centre-forwards who had played for England before him, this was already impressively consistent. The best run of the great G. O. Smith, between 1896 and 1901, was fifteen consecutive caps, and the longest unbroken sequence of Lawton's own hero and master, Dixie Dean, was thirteen between 1927 and 1929. Statistics of this kind are of course always unfair to the players of earlier periods, because in their day international matches were rarer than they are in ours. (Compare the length of time it took G. O. Smith to win his fifteen consecutive caps with the time it took Dean to win his thirteen.) Lawton, however, was only just beginning his assault on these records. No other centre-forward throughout his period was so much the 'automatic choice' for England. After those eight pre-war matches, he played ten times in succession in Wartime Internationals, in seven out of eight Victory Internationals, and in fifteen consecutive post-war England games. Counting them all, over ten years, Lawton played for England forty-eight times, and scored forty-six goals.

These 'Wartime' and 'Victory' matches, played between 1939 and 1946, were not rated as full internationals, but they should not be under-estimated on that account. It is worth remembering that the men who played in them were drawn from a great generation of English footballers. Take, for instance, the team that Lawton described as the best he ever played in, the side that beat Scotland 8–0 in 1943: Swift; Scott, Hardwick; Britton, Cullis, Mercer; Matthews, Carter, Lawton, Hagan, D. Compton. Lawton scored four in that match, including a hat trick in ten minutes. Stanley Matthews had one of his extraordinary games, when no tackle went within feet of him, finished by walking right through on his own and dribbling round the goalkeeper to score the last goal, and ran back to the centre spot applauded by the players of both sides. The famous old footballer Charles Wreford Brown, an England half-back in the 1890s, and by 1943 an England selector, described the match as 'perhaps the greatest combination and team work in the whole history of international football.' Good as this team was, it could not include a number of the other fine players who appeared in England sides during those years; the goalkeepers Bartram, Ditchburn and Williams; the great back Eddie Hapgood; Crayston and Copping among the half-backs, and, among the forwards, Mannion, Shackleton and Mortenson.

There were some players whose football careers were finished or unhappily shortened by the war. Lawton was lucky enough to escape this. When he joined the army he was attached, like many other professionals, to the Army Physical Training Corps, more popularly known as the Footballers' Battalion. This gave him the opportunity to play in Europe and the Middle East, as well as in this country, and it meant he was available for wartime League competitions – first with his own club, Everton, when he was stationed at Birkenhead, and later at Aldershot. As one might expect, some offensive things were said about the footballers in the A.P.T.C. The people who called them 'P.T. Commandos' and 'D-Day Dodgers' would no doubt have been happy if the army had followed its traditional system of classification and put these first-class professionals to work as potato-peelers or lorry-drivers; but if that had happened, some thousands of soldiers and civilians, hungry for the pastimes of peace, would have been deprived of the pleasure of watching them. They made their contribution to 'morale'. As Max Miller used to say, from the stage of the Palladium: 'Who do they want to see, when they've got some time off? Not a lot of old rubbish – stars!'

When the war ended, and the clubs got down to serious thinking about team-building, Chelsea decided they needed a top-class centre-forward. The best in the country – Lawton – cost them £11,500 and, although this seems modest by current standards, it was then the highest fee ever paid. It provoked, as such transactions always have done, outraged letters to the newspapers and a certain amount of derision from the terraces. Lawton's first game for Chelsea was something of a showpiece. The visitors were the famous Moscow Dynamos, and the match was an illuminating experience for most people in this country – the first indication of the high standard of play that had been developing in Russia while, as it were, our backs were turned. The general English attitude was still tolerantly superior – it took the 6–3 win of the Hungarians at Wembley in 1953 to change that – but the crowd were impressed. It was a record crowd, too. The official figure was 82,000 – but that was before the closed gates were broken down, and the other thousands, who had been pushing and complaining outside, flooded in. The result was a 3–3 draw, and Chelsea's third goal was headed in by Lawton, in his own particular grand manner. Those of the Chelsea supporters who were disgruntled about the £11,500 – as if it was their money –

still reserved their judgment until they had seen him in a few League games. They were not disappointed – or maybe the malicious ones were. Lawton played in thirty-four matches that season, and broke the club's individual scoring record in the First Division with twenty-six goals.

Then the trouble began – the newspaper stories about his 'disagreements' with Chelsea, his request for a transfer, the club's refusal to let him go, the talk about arbitration and the Players' Union. There was a new instalment on the back pages every day for weeks. 'We have not received an acceptable offer' the Board of Directors said – but it was rumoured that Arsenal, Blackburn, Derby County, Nottingham Forest and Stoke City were all in the market, and that an offer of £17,000 had in fact been made. This should have been acceptable to anybody, since it would have been a new record. When the situation was finally resolved, it was big news again. Tommy Lawton, the England centre-forward, was going to the Third Division, to Notts County, and they were paying £20,000 for him. The next question was – could a Third Division player keep his place in the England team? He did, for three more internationals and, besides that, unmoved by all the gossip and publicity – much of it unpleasant – he went on playing good, cool, intelligent football, raised the average gate from 9,000 to 35,000, helped the team to win the championship of the Third Division South in 1950, and, with 31 goals in that season, was the top individual scorer in the Division. It was ten years since he had been top scorer in Division One with Everton.

There were plenty of people – especially business men on boards of directors – who had disagreeable things to say about Lawton's hard head for business, but surely no-one could honestly claim that he didn't give value for money. It is worth remembering, too, that this was the period before players at last won the right to negotiate their own contracts. Lawton, who could fill any ground in the country, was expressly forbidden to accept more than £12 a week wages, with £2 for a win, £1 for a draw, and £10 a week in the off season. It was true that he had other income – from a newspaper column, advertising, broadcasting and film appearances – but the basic pay, even then, was still ridiculous. He stayed with Notts County for five years, until 1952, and then the stories began again. What they boiled down to was that Lawton was not happy with

Notts County, and, as the club said, 'he is leaving us at his own request.'

No-one likes hearing of one of their favourite players involved in tedious arguments with people who are in another line of business altogether, but this latest turn of events was good news for some of us devoted connoisseurs who lived in London. Lawton was going to the Second Division, to Brentford – transfer fee, £12,000. We got out our London Transport guides to refresh our memories as to the quickest way to Griffin Park. You can see a First Division team any week in London, but the possibility of Lawton every other Saturday is something else again. It was worth it. Lawton was heavier, more cynical (who wouldn't be?) and he was lying back a little further than he used to; but he was still cool, his judgment of a pass was still superb. He still prowled about watchfully with that rangy, forward-leaning stride, and pounced with deadly quickness on any mistake in the defence; he could still spin on his toe and shoot on the turn; the shot was still terrifyingly hard and directed at the one particular place in the goal that was hardest to reach.

True, from time to time, his impatience with men of lesser ability showed itself. He would watch a bad pass run too far ahead with incredulous disgust, without making any move to follow it. In extreme cases he would stand still, staring at the man who made it, and indicate with his finger the point on the field, somewhat nearer, where it should have gone. 'Get a move on, Lawton!' said the ignorant. We looked at them with loathing. Yet he was still unselfish when it came to making openings, and the men with him were full of interest – stocky, tough Jimmy Bowie, the energetic enthusiastic Billy Dare, and a clever boy who was then new to League Football – Jim Bloomfield. When he had been with Brentford nearly a year, it was announced that Lawton was taking over as team manager. He was thirty-three, and one wondered if that was the first step in a new direction, but he gave it up after nine months or so, and went back to being simply a player.

It seemed that the graph of Lawton's career was curving downward. There would be no more record fees, and the pieces about him in the papers would, one assumed, be smaller as the years went by. Then, suddenly, the headlines were bigger than ever, and the news was astonishing and unexpected. At thirty-four, Lawton was back in the First Division – and with Arsenal. Arsenal had begun the

TOMMY LAWTON 'The mere presence of Lawton made the best and coolest defences uneasy. He was skilful, powerful and dangerous, and one of the great pleasures of watching him was that he looked the part'

SIR STANLEY MATTHEWS 'Once he told a journalist, himself a famous
player, in one of the rare moments when Matthews unburdened
himself, that there was no secret in his play'

1953-54 season as League Champions, but things had gone badly for them in the opening matches, a run of eight without a win. What they decided they needed was the steadying influence and authority of a mature experienced player. This is not the only case where Arsenal have made an unexpected but extremely intelligent choice when faced with such a situation. There was Ronnie Rooke, for instance, and Joe Mercer, who, arriving to deal with a temporary emergency, stayed for eight years.

Lawton did the job he was hired for, and did it well. He was, of course, no longer so fast over the ground as he had been – but he was still a good deal faster than he looked. The leisureliness of his movement was always deceptive. He read the game so well, anticipated so accurately, that whatever he intended to do, he started early. He still moved smoothly through a defence, cutting his way in quarter circles, with his shoulders swaying, controlling the ball with the outside of the foot. He was still hard to reach with a tackle, not easily shaken by a charge.

With Arsenal, one remembers particularly how well he marshalled the line and distributed the ball. The old trick of the short headed pass was still opening gaps for the inside forwards, whose names were now Lishman and Tapscott. When he swept a long forward pass to either wing, his style, if it had lost some of its electric quality, had gained a kind of magnificence. In 1955, he went with the team to Russia. It was not a memorable tour as far as football was concerned – they were beaten 5–0 by his old acquaintances Moscow Dynamo – but for Lawton personally it had its pleasant side. He was in Moscow for his thirty-fifth birthday, and the Russian footballers threw a surprise party for him, with a birthday cake two feet square.

He stayed with Arsenal for three years, and it gave time for the younger talent – plentiful, as usual at Highbury – to settle down and acquire confidence. When his period of usefulness ended, it ended in the Arsenal manner – that is to say without arguments, cheap publicity or recriminations. Tom Whittaker, the manager, told him he would let him know when a good opening offered for a player-manager. When it came – from Kettering Town in the Southern League – Arsenal let him go for £1,000. He made an immediate success of the new job. Kettering were top of their league, with ten points in hand, by Christmas of his first season. The team-building went well – with Whittaker's help – the spirit of the club improved,

E

and there was great enthusiasm for his youth training programme. Then, when he had been there a year, he was unexpectedly offered the job of player-manager, at £2,500 a year, with Notts County, the club he had left, in disagreeable circumstances, five years before. One cannot help feeling – if only he had turned it down.

It was soon apparent that the directors were divided in their opinions as to whether they should engage him, whether they could afford him, whether they could ask the acting manager, Frank Broome, to stand down. The arguments inside the club were given the widest publicity, but still Lawton took the job, and, as one might expect, the engagement was short and unhappy. Notts County dismissed him in 1958, and Lawton announced that he was finished with football.

It is a conventional comment on a player like Lawton – or Stanley Matthews – that he was born a little too soon for his talent to be properly rewarded, not only in money but in esteem. The oldest of speculations about sport is irresistible. Would the giants of another period stand out as great men today, in the late 1960s? It is my own belief that the man who is gifted enough to rise well above others who practise his craft in his own time would also have the ability to adjust himself to change. I cannot believe that a C. B. Fry, a Maurice Tate, a Fred Perry, a Steve Donoghue – or a Tommy Lawton – would be a nonentity in any period. 'We are all worms,' Winston Churchill said, 'but I do believe I am a glow-worm.' There are such people.

The world of football in which Lawton grew up is gone now. It was a period, for one thing, when the superiority of England was rarely questioned. In the forties, any good performance by a visiting international side provoked, on all the back pages, automatic references to 'masters' and 'promising pupils'. The Europeans and the South Americans were in the process of creating the new styles, but it was still 'the English game' that ruled the world. This style, as we think of it now, was simple and direct; hard tackling, solid shoulder-charging, long passing, determined finishing. It was not quite as simple-minded as that, even if later on the Hungarians and the Brazilians did expose the weaknesses of the method. England were the masters of football in the forties, not because of any superiority of system, but because of the moral advantage of her tradition, and, even more, because of the superior talents of her players. The forward line of Matthews, Carter, Lawton, Mannion and Finney, magically transported, at their best, into the 1960s, would have the most highly-organised of modern defences in trouble.

One curious result of the scientific development of football tactics is that the star player, first eclipsed, is now admired and valued again. In the earliest days of football, systems, where they existed at all, were so ill-conceived or ill-executed that the brilliant player – the dribbler, as he then was – simply walked through them. The systems improved, and for a while he faded out. Over the years, the football machines, especially the defensive machines, have become more calculating and efficient. The trained fitness, strength and energy of the players now approaches a maximum – and an equality. We find that in one sense we are thrown back to the earlier period of the brilliant individualists, because only the unexpected can defeat the superbly efficient – and the ability to produce the unexpected, the incalculable, is the characteristic of the gifted individual. For contemporary examples, see George Best, Denis Law, and the Russian Chislenko.

It is true, however, that the footballers of the 1940's tended to be specialists, while now the ideal of the modern game is the all-round, all-purpose footballer. Lawton was a specialist, a goal-scorer – because that was what the game of his day required. The shot, and the header, were *extra* qualities to his outstanding all-round ability. What is required of the 'rotation' footballer that he could not do? He was fast, he was fit, he could read a game, he was intelligent. He could tackle, he could give a pass or move into place to receive one, his ball control was of the very highest order, his reflexes were incredibly quick. One remembers him gratefully as the greatest of centre-forwards – but put Lawton, at twenty-one, in the present company of World Cup competition, in any position on the field, and there is no team anywhere that would not find him formidable as an opponent, or welcome as a power and a delight in their own side.

There is one not entirely unimportant footnote that should be added, in a period that produces too much violence, theatre and brutality. Lawton probably took more punishment in the way of tripping, unscrupulous tackling, hammering and bumping than any man of his period. The specialist centre-forward was the natural target for it. No one ever saw Lawton retaliate, or deliberately foul anyone. That he should lose his temper or be sent off was unthinkable. In over twenty years, he never did, and he never was.

FOUR

Sir Stanley Matthews
by Albert Barham

SIR STANLEY MATTHEWS, CBE? queried the man who stands at the gate of the year. 'He's still "our Stan" in the Potteries whether he's got handles front and back of his name or not.' And 'our Stan' as remarkable for his elusiveness as for his longevity as England's finest forward – and to many the greatest in the world – stays where he was particularly idolised – in the Potteries. Until July he was general manager of Port Vale. But now Stanley Matthews advises. 'And it's far more wearing mentally than ever it was for me as an international player. Still when I leave Port Vale at night and drive back home to Blackpool – it's only an hour and a half away – I leave all my troubles behind. I put on my blinkers and relax at home.'

Vale Park in Burslem is no shining memorial, the club is on the bottom rungs of the ladder of the Football League, but this is the heart of the area where the legend of Matthews is still as great as the man – and the man as great as the legend: the Knight and the Commander are but the outward and visible signs of reward for a man who is still the finest ambassador Soccer ever had.

Here stays Stanley Matthews, rising fifty-four in February, still the superb athlete, a wizard who had the world by the ears, and who is still in demand as a player. Already he has been asked to make a summer tour of Zambia, to exhibit again skills in Winnipeg and to thrill once more the Dutch as he did three decades ago.

To the youngsters there are only tales all the richer for the re-telling, and the fuzzy films of the past: to the older follower of football those performances of Matthews on England's wing are still caught in the camera of memories – and who of those who ever saw him cannot still produce from the mind's file a whole series of sharp pictures of Matthews in all his glory?

But the past is not for Stanley Matthews. 'Things went right for me; and they went well' he admits diffidently 'but I don't look back . . . not at all the photographs . . . you can get old looking at the trophies. People can get to mope if they live in the past. Those days are gone . . . gone. What's the use of thinking of all the money the footballers make now compared with thirty years ago? Good luck to them if they can earn it – they deserve it. I like the present, not the past.'

Yet how can one really forget that past? Remember England's

match against Czechoslovakia in 1937 at White Hart Lane? . . .
Matthews caressing the ball between his feet, tantalising, waiting,
luring, from an unusual position of inside forward? For England
had to reorganise after the injury to Crayston. And from this new
position, Matthews scored three goals, the last in the dying minutes
to give England victory by 5-4.

He was a goal taker then but he became a goal maker. Remember Matthews demoralising the Irish at Manchester? And the Scots
at Wembley? Remember Matthews' Cup Final of 1953? Life's
rich memories are recaptured in moments such as those as he
outwitted the foreign backs, and his triumphant recall after years
in the international wilderness to play and confound Brazil. Then
he was forty-one, and mighty proud of it. And the emotional farewell against a team drawn from the pages of the world of football's
Debrett?

And here he is on the park with his 'boys.' There is still that
superb balance; the immeasurable self-confidence as he brings
down the ball from the most difficult pass and gathers it under
control in a sliver of a second . . . then away, slowly at first,
spidery legs stroking the ball from foot to foot, slight body hunched
at the shoulders, shirt flapping untidily, leaning over the ball . . .
beckoning, daring, drawing defenders with the magnetism of his
feet. And having lured and committed his opponent, unnerving him
by showing him the ball and rolling it away with the sole of his
foot, suddenly Matthews is away. A swerve of the body leaves the
back pinned on one foot – the wrong way to tackle – a flick of the
ball with the inside or outside of the foot and he is gone, with an
acceleration over twenty yards that no forward yet has matched.
Even with thirty years of sorcery behind it, defenders, the young
and the older, more mature players, fall for it and are left leaden-
footed and bereft of recovery.

When his opponent wavers Matthews senses his chance, so utterly
confident is he in his own power to outwit him. Having done so,
an opportunity is so seldom wasted with a bad pass. Over they
come, floating cunningly, precisely and just out of reach of the
goalkeeper's groping fingers. That was the stuff which thrilled the
world. It is still an experience, shared more often these days, by the
boys from Port Vale, and by the followers of football in distant
parts.

One can recall a famous back who claimed he had an infallible system for stopping Matthews. It never worked, and like a man, the defender ruefully admitted it. 'He didn't look at me or the ball but just where he was going to put it. And on a pinpoint too. He got you on the wrong foot and he was off. Like a flash. Unstoppable. And that burst of speed. It was incredible.'

How was it all done? Stanley Matthews is essentially a shy, reserved man. To him a laugh is an indulgence. The drawn features crease and a smile is nudged over the edge into audibility. 'I wanted to destroy players. Not physically but psychologically. For then they lost confidence. They lost their energy quickly . . . and without energy they can do nothing. So many players put their heads down and moved themselves right into trouble. Like a tennis player, a good one, you can get a picture in the mind. You know and can sense the flight of the ball. And you have the time, your opponent has not. You can see where you are going to go and where you are going to put the ball. It's all done by experience and that is some-thing that you cannot really teach to anyone.

'It's so important to beat a back on the outside . . . not on the inside. Never go inside. I always went outside a back when I could . . . making sure he thought I was going the other way . . . and down the touchline. And at the byeline you can pinpoint a centre or cut the ball back. No one can get caught offside and ruin a move when you do this. Running inside all the time only gets everybody into a muddle . . . congests everything. And if you shoot the ball can so easily curl wide or be blocked. Now, if you go down the wing the goalkeeper doesn't know whether to stay at the far post or to move to the near one. He's confused too. You've done your job and that's the aim of it all.'

Once he told a journalist, himself a famous player, in one of the rare moments when Matthews unburdened himself, that there was no secret in his play – that gifted style studied so assiduously and copied without real success throughout the world. 'Yet honestly I don't think I could do it in cold blood,' he said, when asked for a demonstration. 'It just comes out of me under pressure.'

He used to be more of a goal scorer in his early days with Stoke City but then decided that a winger who made chances for his three inside men was of far greater value to his team. There is much to be said for that argument. There is much to be said for a winger who can hold the ball until there is an opening. But it is not the whole of the argument. If it were, the 'old-fashioned' winger, dribbling the ball down the touchline would be a far more common sight than it is. The method of Matthews, in modern football, would require a special kind of skill which few ever attain. In fact it requires Matthews, a type of genius which is a football tactic in itself.

It is a style which he created for himself, the rare skill, the confidence stemming from superb fitness. That was, if not bred into him by his father, at least instilled in his memory. For Jack Matthews, the 'Fighting Barber from Hanley,' a featherweight and not much heavier than Matthews junior, insisted on physical conditioning. It was Jack Matthews who made his children stand before the open window breathing deeply; lift bar-bells; and walk the two miles to school and back every day. Lifting bar-bells certainly did not bring to Stanley Matthews a great physique: he is inclined towards hollow-chestedness. But it instilled into him a discipline for fitness. Indeed fitness became a fetish: yet Stanley Matthews has been amply repaid for it. Today, still abstemious, he is fitter than men a dozen years his junior.

Those early lessons have so amply repaid him, and the skills developed as he kicked a ball round on his long journeys home from school. In the Potteries where good footballers were fashioned at almost every street corner there was early promise from Stanley Matthews. Once in a school match he scored ten goals – as centre-half. He became a schoolboy international outside-right but his career in football was only begun when maternal connivance overcame paternal objections. As soon as he left school in 1930 he joined Stoke City for £1 a week. He was a regular member of the League team at seventeen and an international at nineteen, gaining the first of his caps then and the forty-seventh and last in a memorable match against Brazil twenty-two years later. For three decades the full fury of erratic publicity blew across him and his career. He was unmoved by it. Trends and tactics seemed to him then of but passing interest, or he was too shy and retiring to command them for so long in his career.

'I was slow, so slow when I was young. At Stoke they told me so, too. But as you get older, experience naturally makes you quicker. All boys of fifteen are slow, I suppose, but I practised every day this burst of speed over thirty yards.' Indeed he trained throughout his career far, far harder of his own volition, than any trainer would have asked him to.

There are perhaps a few people still who recall an entry in a notebook which has long since lost its shine: 'Matthews had a fair game. Could make the grade. But at the moment is not the man we are looking for.'

A few weeks later one word – 'Concur' – was scrawled as a post-script and the assessment of Stanley Matthews was scored through in pencil. The directors who 'concurred' are now no longer of this world; the scout who produced the report is now a forgotten man though, in mitigation, he said before anonymity swallowed him: 'Anyone can make mistakes.'

Mistakes were always being made about Stanley Matthews. 'Hell, he'll never stand the rigours of the game.' 'There are too many pitfalls for one so slight' are but two of the thoughts spoken aloud by League managers at the time of the emergence of Matthews.

It was strange, in view of the latent flair he had for the great occasion, that he should have begun so poorly for England. No one could say his second international against Italy was a great success. 'I saw Matthews in the Inter-League match', wrote a critic at the time, 'play just as moderately. Perhaps he lacks the big match temperament. He was slow and hesitant.'

Matthews knew he was slow and was correcting that in his own way and, by the season of 1937, had really established himself. That was against Czechoslovakia at White Hart Lane. There the three goals, each a shot with the left foot, were sufficient answer to the critics who said he could not score goals. That, as time went on, he became more and more interested in creating opportunities for others was, perhaps, the sign of maturity. The following year proved it when he bewitched the Irish at Manchester and five goals came from his touches. His popularity grew with his ability.

It is possible with most players to look back over their record and say: 'That was the match: *that* was the real peak of his career.' But not with Matthews. Ask at random a dozen of his most devoted admirers. All will pick a different game. There was the match against Germany in 1955 – the corresponding match seventeen years before; the defeat of Scotland, also in 1955, the day Duncan Edwards played for the first time for England – and Matthews was an international even before he was born.

The Cup Final 1953 is perhaps remembered with more sentiment than many an international. Stanley Matthews' Cup winners' medal had become as mythical as Gordon Richards's winning Derby mount. It was his third and positively last appearance in the Cup Final, as everyone suspected. But that was with Blackpool, and how had he got to that seaside club? As long ago as 1938 Stoke was split by controversy. Matthews had recovered from injury and the City management, loth to change a winning team, suggested that Matthews should play in the reserves. Matthews felt his game would lose its edge in the reserves. He asked for a transfer. He was worth a place in anyone's League side he said. And the result was that a great hall was hired and filled by those who demanded that Matthews should stay with City. 'Matthews must not go' screamed the banners placed along the way to the hall. A city in torment was reprieved. Matthews stayed.

In 1947 almost the same set of circumstances were repeated. This time Matthews did go. He had stipulated that he would consider only one club, Blackpool, with whom he had played as a guest during the war. And so to Blackpool he went – for a fee of £11,500 – to play alongside Mortenson and Johnston. There he played three Cup Finals, the last of which is the most remembered one of all at Wembley. It was one of Matthews' finest hours. He stood there before the Queen; calm, certainly the most unmoved of any of the players: slightly hunched and we said: 'He looks his age.' Yet, if he did, he was unequalled. But when Blackpool were 3-1 down with twenty minutes to play it seemed that his greatest ambition, that of a Cup winners' medal, would be denied him. When he had missed them in the past he said simply 'Pity, I would have liked to have won one and given it to my son.'

At that point in the final Matthews really played at his greatest. He roamed the field after the ball. Instinct, rhythm, excitement were all there as he created, with one of those runs to the byeline, the famous centre which curls out of the goalkeeper's reach. Mortenson scored from it. Three minutes from time with all England who could watch on television willing him on, Blackpool scored the equaliser. Again it was Mortenson. Matthews, as the players leapt and cavorted around him, opened his mouth, raised himself, half-lifted his arms. Was Matthews going to have a little celebration as well? Then the training and discipline of a lifetime drew him back. He just clapped his hands, as if to say 'Let's get on, there is still time.'

And time there was. Just. There was less than thirty seconds to go when Taylor pushed a pass once again to Matthews. He took it without changing stride. Banks came to tackle him and was left behind. Barrass came from the packed goalmouth to block his way. Matthews feinted again and wheeled almost to the byeline and the defenders wheeled with him. He cut the ball back, hard and fast and there was Perry, the outside-left, cutting in to find the only gap in Bolton's defence. Blackpool had won the cup and Matthews his coveted medal. It had been his day.

But for years he was on the shelf as far as international selection was concerned. How could one explain to the excitable South Americans, the voluble French, the Italians, whose impassioned appeals with the hands speak a language of their own, when they posed such ingenuous questions – 'Matthews? No, then you have someone better?' Perhaps Finney was as great in any company and in another style, but that is another story.

Matthews was a world figure wherever he went, if not for England then on his jaunts giving exhibition tours in the summer. He was fêted wherever he went. Yet the irony of his career is that he never became a rich man by it. He was always wary of exploiting his name, though when he did, he did so shrewdly. And even though his earnings, supplemented as they were by his additional sidelines, were higher than the average professional of his day they were still paltry when compared with the professionals in other sports.

Sooner or later almost all the international players have an urge to write their memoirs. Stanley Matthews was no exception. Yet when he asked his father in the summer of 1939 for his advice, young Stanley's boyish enthusiasm was rudely shattered. 'Who do you think you are, "Fanny" Waldon?' Jack Matthews chided him kindly: 'No, Stan, wait a year or two. What folk will bother to sit down and read the comings and goings of a lad of twenty-three. When you have really lived. When you really have a story worth telling . . . then's the time to get down and write it.' So *Feet First*, his first book, the one he wanted to write when he had been capped seventeen times had been in and out of nine countries, was delayed until long after the war. By then Jack Matthews had died. Yet his advice was so worth while. Matthews by then really had a story to tell. His second book, *The Stanley Matthews Story* followed in 1960. But is was his performances one followed rather than his writing, which caused critics to blow hot and cold.

For years he was plagued by a knee injury, one that bothers him at times to this day. Hard grounds were the bane of his life then, just as hard shale surfaces are now, and I recall one Cup match at Southampton on a frosty surface when he teetered along for all the world as though he had blisters on every toe. Those were his off days, very few and far between, for he gave all his effort for his sides.

How many of the 85,000 who saw him break Eddie Hapgood's record of forty-four international matches could have realised just how close he was to missing that game against Belgium at Wembley? It was a record which might well have stood for another year, for the old knee injury kept Matthews out of the England team to play Scotland at Hampden Park in the following April and he had to drop out of the first two internationals of the 1946-47 season.

Prior to the match against Belgium, Stanley Matthews had been on night duty with the R.A.F. It was bitter weather and Matthews caught a chill. Bill Voisey dosed him but even so: 'I could not have dragged myself from bed had it not been for that record.' On that bleak January day, however, he was able to warm up in comfort for then, for the first time, England wore track suits . . . though they had been in the F.A. stores for years. It was the beginning, too, of the use of luminous flags by linesmen – and quite effective they proved, for the fog rolled down. 'Young' Billy Wright had been chosen to play at inside-right, but because of the injury to Frank Soo, he played at right-half. It was the beginning also of Wright's long reign in England's half-back line. 'Frank Swift never had a quieter afternoon for England than he did that day though Daenen, his Belgian counterpart, only 5ft 6in high, had tremendous agility. He needed it for Lawton and Pye were in great form.' From the kaleidoscope of so many memories it is difficult for Matthews to relive the greatest of his games.

'One of the most enjoyable was the one the R.A.F. played in Lisbon, but I have not made up my mind whether my greatest game for England was against Ireland at Old Trafford in November 1938 when England won 7–0, or against Czechoslovakia in December 1937. 'Against Ireland I claimed one of the goals myself, but I had the pleasure of helping that grand little inside-right Willie Hall of Spurs to score five in succession and so set up a record for a full England international.

'Certainly it was my happiest match, because Hall had been my partner a week earlier against the Scottish League and I was sick to think I had been accused of starving him out of the game. The thought that Hall might lose his cap against Ireland was a source of misery to me. I could have danced around when Hall was selected'.

Oddly enough, five years later, when England beat Wales 8–3 in a Wartime international, the sporting critics accused the rest of the England team of freezing Matthews out of the game. But, like Hall, Matthews was quite unaware of the 'freeze.'

Stan Cullis said that it was a counter to the plan of Ted Robbins the Welsh F.A.'s secretary to stop Matthews. Hughes and Burgess watched Matthews, said Cullis, and Carter, Walsh and Hagan had plenty of room and time to move. It led to one of the great controversies of the time. Even the F.A. were involved. They issued a statement saying that letters had been received from some of the England team deprecating suggestions that there was even the slightest jealousy of Matthews, nor was there any attempt to ostracize him. And Matthews was unmoved by that too. He said simply 'Stan Cullis was one of the greatest and best skippers I have ever played under. He gave the team a superiority complex before we even went on the field. It was almost as good as a goal in hand.'

Matthews was never distinguished by his heading of the ball, indeed one can still recall the buzz of the crowd when he did. 'And no-one, after the three goals I scored against Czechoslovakia – my only hat-trick in international matches – could call me a goal scoring winger. When I got a goal after that it was "news", a point which I offer in my defence to charges sometimes made against me that I am a selfish player. When I ran three-quarters the length of the field to score England's eighth goal at Manchester against Scotland in October 1943, it was my first goal for five years.'

'My worst matches? Well there was that match against Switzerland in Zurich in 1938 when Lehmann, a dance-band leader and left-back for the Swiss, played me out of the game for so much of the match that I might as well have stood there and yodelled and waited for the echo from the mountains. Neither shall I forget the poor match I had against the Germans at Tottenham in 1935. But my three worst games were all played in a few weeks of one season before the war against a Leicester City back called Maurice Reeday. A more difficult back I never opposed. It began in a League match the week before we were due to play Leicester in the Cup. I had not even heard of the player before that. And later I grabbed a programme to find out just who my tormentor had been. I played in the same fashion that had taken me along quite nicely against defenders with big reputations. He began by robbing me of the ball quite easily and the longer the game went on the easier it was for him. I changed my tactics and nothing shook him off. I changed positions and Reeday followed me. I was so fed up with my own failure that in desperation I said to him "Haven't you got a home to go to?" He just grinned and replied "Yes, but it won't blow away until the game's finished!" I worked out a plan to beat him in the Cup tie. That failed, too, though we did draw; but the replay was just the same and we were beaten.'

I suppose one of the sweetest victories for Matthews was that over Germany 6–3 in Berlin, in May 1938. Not only was there vindication of his poor showing when they had met earlier, but it was also more satisfying than the defeat of the Italians at Highbury. Perhaps, too, there was more than a little patriotism at a time when Europe was simmering under the twin threats of Mussolini and Hitler. Matthews recalls a tall distinguished man stepping into the dressing-room afterwards and saying casually: 'You have done a good job for England this afternoon.' It was Sir Neville Henderson, British Ambassador. And Matthews was proud. For he had a great game. He gained some satisfaction from outwitting Muezenberg the German left-back who had blotted him out of the game in the only previous match against Germany, three years earlier. Not that any revenge was ever sought by Matthews, but Muezenberg had slowed beyond his wildest hopes and especially did Matthews want to do well that day. It was the afternoon when the England team had to give the Nazi salute. The Germans, 100,000 strong, gave England a generous applause as they entered the field. 'It was only a whisper compared with the great roar when the Germans appeared. But even in that noisy crowd it did not prevent me hearing a few pipey voices from behind the goal "Let 'em have it England". It was a great encouragement.'

A year after that triumph in Berlin came the F.A.'s last foreign tour for seven years, to Italy and the Balkans, an enjoyable trip for Matthews, yet one which, owing to the tenseness of the political situation and the delicate state of the balance of Europe, was almost called off after consultations with the Government.

Alex James was the greatest footballer Stanley Matthews ever saw. 'His dribbling was superb,' he writes in his autobiography. And praise of that description from a man who prided himself on his ball control is praise indeed. 'It was not always what he did but what he did not do which caused so much trouble to opposing defences. That spud nose and bushy eyebrows turned up in the most unexpected places. Alex was a genius of tactics.'

Tom Finney 'my old friendly rival' kept him out of the England team for a while and, for a time, they prospered together on opposite wings. 'A clever winger', was Finney, 'I had no grouse against him. He was a fine footballer' he commented at the time when Finney established himself in England's team, and the critics openly said that he had come to stay at the expense of Matthews. But it was 'a happy team which did a good job for England.' And it was a good one, too, for who does not remember with pride the performances of Carter, Mortenson and Lawton and Mannion and behind them Swift, Scott, Hardwick, Wright, Franklin? Swift was, in Matthews's eyes, the greatest of all goalkeepers; Cullis one of the greatest of centre-halves; and Farrow, of Blackpool one of the greatest wing-halves never to have played for England.

But no-one yet has persuaded Matthews to pick the team of greatest ever players. 'Comparisons between players of different periods are absurd,' he says. 'It is like arguing whether Dempsey was better than Sullivan as a fighter. You could argue for a year without proving a point.'

When England passed him over in their periodic switches, Stanley Matthews said he felt he was tasting some of the sour grapes after years of savouring the sweet things of life: 'I felt that the publicity given to my troubles with Stoke City had done my cause no good, and I was a little hurt at the fickleness of folk who professed one minute to be friends and the next were spreading round the word that I was out for good.'

However, in one of those bad periods through which all of us pass, there was comfort indeed from Billy Meredith. It was Meredith's record of fifty-one caps which Matthews was hoping to surpass. 'It was a wonderful record, for they were gained in full internationals and caps were not awarded during the war years.' And, in this 'my bad season of '46' it was Meredith who came up to him to wish him luck in beating the record: 'You'll be back before the season is out' he said. And he was brought back. He played for Great Britain against the Rest of Europe the week after

F

England had beaten France. Nine years before he had played for England against the Rest of Europe at Highbury 'but this was more important for the team was selected from England, Ireland, Wales and Scotland. It was a special match to celebrate the return of the F.A. to F.I.F.A. after a break of eighteen years.'

Having returned to the fold, England played in the World Cup. Matthews was in the party which went to Chile. And what a disaster that was, though Matthews sat out the matches against Chile and the defeat by U.S.A. by 1–0. 'I sat with bowed head until the players had left the field. I never thought I would live to see this. As I raised my head to look around me later I felt a pain in most of my fingers. I looked down at my hands and saw spots of blood on the palms. I had been so tense in the closing minutes of the match that I had dug my finger nails into my flesh without at the time feeling a thing', he wrote in his book.

'I can't say I jumped for joy when I heard I was selected to play against the Spaniards. For one reason I had been a spectator at the Chile and United States matches and I had noticed that the will to win was sadly lacking in the England team. I blame this on the pre-match talk on playing tactics that had been introduced for the first time by our team manager. You just cannot tell star players how they must play and what they must do when they are on the field in an international match. You must let them play their natural game.'

This was the match in which Matthews said he 'broke out in a cold sweat as the closing minutes came and quickly passed. I thought it mustn't happen –we must not lose this match. We lost it. England, masters of soccer, had failed even to qualify for the World Cup.'

Matthews did not agree with Walter Winterbottom, England's manager's team changes, or his tactics. Matthews firmly believed at the time that Winterbottom was trying to change to the continental style of play. 'I, myself, believe that we should stick to the style that brought us great success in the past – which is our natural style; the English style.'

Modesty is no false mask. Stanley Matthews lives simply. For a while he and his wife ran a small hotel in Blackpool. At his home, The Grange, where the garden was almost all lawn, there was another side to be learned of Matthews the family man, with a daughter and son, both now lawn tennis players of no mean ability.

'Are you playing tonight, Stan?' the question used to be asked over the garden wall. 'Yes, six o'clock' said Stan, and the visitor might be forgiven for thinking he had been told of a League match he had forgotten. But it was, in fact, the time of the Matthews's organised five-a-side family games on the lawn, played every day the weather was suitable.

What a contrast this was to Matthews the international ... getting on in years and around whom controversy raged. 'I never knew when I had a good game, players used to say "Stan, you played darned well today." I didn't know. I couldn't see myself. You only know on those occasions that you have conditioned yourself right and you have the strength to get the ball. You know only that things are right.'

There were the rumblings when he was chosen to play against the Rest of the World in the Football Association's 90th anniversary celebrations. They continued when he was chosen in 1957 to play against Brazil. He was, said the critics, too old, yet here was another game turned by Matthews from probable defeat into victory by his virtuosity. 'Too old' he said in a most unusual moment of disgust after the game. 'Do you know there have been times when I have wanted to tear the paper across.' For he was, and is, proud, and justly so: reserved, too: that statement was untypical of him. The principal impression he gives off the field is an unwillingness to talk about himself.

Eventually, and perhaps inevitably, Matthews went back to Stoke City. 'It was the greatest period of my career – the one in which Stoke gained promotion to the First Division and I played in almost all the forty-eight matches. Things went well for me then.'

The greatest satisfaction he ever gained was showing that he was not a 'write off.' 'I knew in my own mind that I could still do it. No-one can tell you what you feel like. I knew I was on a winner. Playing up to the age of fifty was a great personal satisfaction. Not only that, but also because I knew that I was not being carried. If I had been I would have packed up there and then.'

But to many, when he went back to Stoke to play in the Second Division, it was an affront. It was something that never should have happened. Not for Matthews's sake perhaps, but for his critics. It reminded them too poignantly that the idols grow old like the rest of us. You could see heads shake and lips formed the words: 'He's not as good as he was: Is any man? It's the same for idolised individuals as it is for the mass. Yet men like Matthews are expected to rise with a triumphant whoosh of a rocket, burst into a glittering display and disappear while the memory retains only the most vivid moments. That was why so often he was told to retire. After all, most of the gods in the other chosen sports retired at the peak of their fame and fortune . . . Marciano, Fangio, Bradman, Gordon Richards. Some stayed on. Borotra was one, Joe Louis another. And did Louis lose much of his public acclaim because he had to fight again to appease the taxman?

Did Matthews suffer by continuing to play League Football? Of course he didn't. 'I don't think in terms of my reputation,' he said at the time of the controversy. 'I do not see why I should retire in a blaze of glory. No-one in the world can tell me when to retire. It's when I lose my enthusiasm – that will be the day.' And that day has yet to come. Does it really matter that now he plays against non-league sides in England, so long as he gets enjoyment from it?

For enjoyment there has always been. 'I can still play ninety minutes anytime. I train just as hard as ever I did,' he said recently. 'A match doesn't cause me any problems. I played in Czechoslovakia twice in two days and everything was all right. It was not too much for me. I know I can play – and not badly either. My experience puts me in that position. Some things do not always go right. But where a young player – and there are not many dedicated to fitness these days – will have one good game in four or five, an experienced player will have a much higher proportion of good games and the others will not be bad, fair perhaps, but not bad. That's what experience does for you. I reckon I am always at my best in the last twenty-five minutes of a game rather than in the opening twenty. I suppose being fit leads one to be a strong finisher.'

Perhaps he is able to finish strongly, in part, because he is expertly shod. He was the pioneer among those who sought a rejection of the old-fashioned football boots and the heavily guarded legs. 'Men in soft plimsolls are faster than men wearing boots' he said simply.

'I always have been most particular about my boots. I like to have about four pairs. In the old days they were the lightest in the world, and I always liked new boots. I liked the shine on them. You could look at the shine – as you do with ordinary shoes – and it does something to you; it makes you proud; it makes you more alive.' It is no surprise that one of Stanley Matthews's enterprises was as advisor to a manufacturer of football boots.

The present era is one of eruption, tantrums and temperament among players on the field. Matthews was never one to show emotion. He was also never a player to retaliate, no matter how great the provocation. He was subject to harsh body checking in an age when it was the form to shoulder charge heavily (but, of course, only when his opponents could reach him). He stayed unflappable, coldly aloof. Once, in particular, at Wembley, a Yugoslav left-back became desperate. He had been made to look a fool by Matthews. He had lunged at him and missed. In desperation he stopped Matthews at last – by clinging to his knees. Matthews got up with not a change in the facial expression. As far as he was concerned, the opponent was finished. 'He had lost his concentration, and thus was himself lost' he said. 'What really is the point in retaliating, either? Players must keep control of themselves. If they do not, they let themselves down and not only themselves but their team, their club and their supporters. And, as for spitting at an opponent . . . what could be more degrading?'

This refusal to be ruffled earned Stanley Matthews the commendation of the football administrators, and rightly so. A resolution was presented to him as an example of his real sportsmanship. 'Never at any time in his career as a Football League player was he guilty of an act, on or off the field, which could have brought the game or the League into disrepute.' Matthews, at this time, in spite of his protestations 'It's my life, I love the game. Why should I retire' was approaching the age when men are honoured for their services. It is the twilight age, the age of indulgence, the age also of chivalry. The City of Stoke in 1963 made 'our Stan' a freeman. There were no big parades. There were no frenzied crowds . . . just a few relations and Stoke team colleagues to applaud him and what he stood for.

The tributes were handsome, none undeserved. Stoke's usually blunt speechmakers called him 'The master craftsman'; 'The perfect gentleman on and off the field'; 'One of Stoke's most illustrious sons'. 'Our Stan' was overwhelmed by it all. A little nervously he rose and quietly said 'My roots are planted on a football field here in Stoke. They have blossomed into the fairest flower I know.' There surely was a touch of the sentimental, for back in 1935 Stanley Matthews married Elizabeth Vallence, the daughter of Stoke City's trainer. And in 1963 he was knighted . . . and spent the season hoping to play against Manchester United in the fourth round of the Cup.

For all his assertions that he does not look back, can there not be in him, as there is in all his supporters all over the world – for many knew of Matthews though they knew nothing of football – a little nostalgia in that match organised as a testimonial by his wellwishers? The greatest of their time played in that International XI – Yashin, Schnellinger, Pluskal. Popluhar, Masopust, Kubala, Di Stefano, Puskas. Dennis Howell, now the Minister responsible for Sport was the referee and, on that night of April 29 1963, Matthews was borne in triumph from the field at Stoke on the shoulders of Yashin and Puskas.

He wrote his autobiographies. *Feet First* and *The Stanley Matthews Story* and through them echoed the triumphant theme of the taming of age.

'I say with the greatest confidence to any young professional footballer who is reaching his twenty-first birthday: get this into your head, that you have a good twenty years of football in you.' He had little thought of turning to the managerial side of the game until approached by Jackie Mudie from Port Vale. Mudie and Matthews had worked alongside each other at Blackpool. So they did at Vale Park.

'I try now to pass on my skills to the young boys here. You cannot teach the older men in the game in the same manner. But it all takes time. It's so long before the results give satisfaction. The problem is that when one does get a batch of boys, so many reach a plateau of achievement and go no further. Some others tend to blossom later. You've got to have a lot of patience.'

I play in Port Vale's friendly matches against the non-League clubs. I find that getting the young player playing with me is so much better than trying to coach from the touchline.

'If I can produce a few good players I shall be happy and lucky. And I look forward to another five years playing and giving exhibitions – no, perhaps that is looking just too far ahead – anyway to several years.' And that's as fine a philosophy as any for a man to whom football was not as much a mystery as he was to football. That, for him, was just a series of facets each of which had to be painstakingly perfected.

Now that he has the power to relax and enjoy life, you may find him where you would expect to find any father – watching his son with a critical eye. Stanley Matthews, himself no mean lawn tennis player in the past, can often be seen, a slight, huddled figure, watching Stanley Matthews junior competing at tournaments throughout Britain. That Stanley Matthews the lawn tennis player has not reached the heights of greatness in his sport as did his father is no great worry to Stanley Matthews the elder. 'The great thing is that he enjoys the game,' he said. Enjoyment, after all, is one of the great blessings. And that the Matthews have.

FIVE

Willie Woodburn
by Hugh McIlvanney

THE PHOTOGRAPH on the fading page of the newspaper files might date from the Thirties. It shows two men stepping from the bare doorway of a Glasgow office building. Three strides in front is the older of the two, his thin face grim under a hat with a large crown and a floppy brim. He is wearing a baggy double-breasted suit. The trousers of the younger man are out-landishly wide, his jacket is open, exposing a striped club tie. He has his coat swung casually over his left shoulder, in the manner of someone who has taken a walk on the prom and found the sun warmer than he had expected. But his face, too, is drawn, his eyes cast down towards the large toecaps of his shoes.

The date of the scene fossilised in the back numbers of the national press is September 14th, 1954 and the man with the coat is Willie Woodburn. Far from taking a carefree walk, he is making a humiliating and irrevocable exit from football, the game that has been his life since he was a schoolboy, in which he has won many honours and the reputation of being one of the two or three greatest centre-halves Britain has ever produced. The late summer sun is shining on the shabby buildings in Carlton Place, Glasgow, but Woodburn carries with him the permanent chill of the most sen-sational sentence ever passed by the Referee Committee of the Scottish Football Association. Meeting in secret to consider the latest in a series of violent misdemeanours by Woodburn, the six members of the Committee had voted to suspend Woodburn *sine die*, without limit. At the time the impression created was that their decision was unanimous but subsequently it emerged that three of the judges had been disposed to apply a limit to the punish-ment, to fix a definite date for the condemned man's return to the game. In the end it was left to the chairman, Mr. John Robbie of Aberdeen, to give a casting vote and he declared the punishment *sine die*. The same calamity had overtaken other players but never before had one of such distinction been involved.

Woodburn was thirty-four, so clearly his best years were behind him, but he had always been in exceptional physical condition. Even now, on the brink of fifty, tall and straight with a waist trim enough to shame men twenty years younger, he emanates a physical vitality that persuades those who meet him that he could still strip and do a job for Rangers or Scotland. We know it is an illusion but it is almost as compelling as that which accompanies

Jack Dempsey in boxing. Dempsey is well into his seventies but he is an eternally contemporary figure and when he takes his magnetic, virile presence into the training camp of a modern champion many who see him find themselves possessed by the ludicrous conviction that if he took off his street clothes, put on the gloves and went into the ring, he would be no worse than even money to come out on top. In football terms, there is something of the same magic about Woodburn.

In 1954 there was nothing illusory about the belief that he was fit to go on playing for several seasons. The older man in that newspaper picture had no doubts. Scot Symon had just been appointed manager of Rangers when the Woodburn crisis developed. Writing of the implications of the disaster ten years afterwards, Symon indicated a depth of concern that was not obscured by the occasional intrusion of melodrama in his prose. 'When the door of the Referee Committee Room opened at last and Willie came out, one look at his face was enough to tell me the verdict. "That's it all finished," he shrugged. His words carried their own meaning. My feelings were immediate and instant. For Willie. For Rangers. I felt as if "The Castle" which once perched so proudly on top of the Ibrox grandstand, had come tumbling to the ground around my ears."

'When I had taken over the managership of Rangers a few weeks before I was well aware that it was a big job – with equally big problems. Age had caught up with several star players. The team was in a period of transition and a lot of rebuilding would have to be done. But there was one great consolation. There was still that masterful, dominating personality at centre-half who would be the sheet anchor of my new team . . . Willie was a football manager's ideal centre-half. I could entrust all thoughts of defensive play to him. Willie knew exactly what had to be done on the field. I reckoned that he had another two or three seasons as a Scotland and Rangers player left . . . Looking back, Woodburn's suspension threw me out of gear more than the loss of any other player who has been under my control."

Of course, Symon had known that Woodburn's punishment would be stiff. The seriousness of the latest offence and the record of previous convictions made that inevitable. Though the manager-player relationship had scarcely begun, Symon had known Woodburn for a long time and he had witnessed at close quarters the accumulation of the big man's troubles. He was a spectator in the enclosure at Parkhead in 1938 when Woodburn, as a precocious 19-year-old, played in his first Rangers-Celtic match against one of the most formidable sides ever to wear the green and white hoops: Kennoway; Hogg, Morrison; Geatons, Lyon, Paterson; Delaney, McDonald, Crum, Divers, Murphy. In that game Symon saw evidence of the impetuosity that was to grow so much later into a menace that would destroy Woodburn's career. With the score 1–1, Jimmy Delaney challenged Rangers goalkeeper Jerry Dawson and Woodburn moved in to shoulder the winger out of the way. Willie Lyon gave Celtic the lead from the penalty and soon afterwards Lyon came upfield again to score with a free-kick awarded for a foul by Woodburn on Malcolm McDonald at the edge of the area. The encouragement of those goals set Celtic going and they slaughtered Rangers 6–2. Symon, swaying in the crowded enclosure, had his own troubles (in the crush he missed a step and aggravated an ankle injury) but he had time to sympathise with the young defender whose blunders had made the day a personal disaster. Rangers at that time were, of course, managed by the legendary autocrat Bill Struth and he was the last man to ignore such lapses. However, Struth's strictures and homilies were comparatively restrained. 'You're far too impetuous,' he told Woodburn. 'The man who never made a mistake never made anything. But most of a centre-half's work is in the penalty area and you can't afford to make mistakes there. You've still got this juvenile habit of holding the ball and inviting trouble. All we expect of you here is that you clear your lines. Leave the wing-halves to play football.'

Woodburn found himself able to absorb only a diluted version of that advice. Though his game developed a striking economy, and he always sought to play with a classic simplicity, he remained very much a footballing centre-half. Sadly, he also remained a physically impulsive one and the problem grew as he got older. In August, 1948, he was ordered off after a violent exchange with Davie Mathie, the Motherwell centre-forward, and subsequently was suspended for fourteen days. On March 7, 1953, he was sent off for a foul on Billy McPhail of Clyde and was banned for twenty-one days. September 26, 1953, saw him ordered off in the Rangers-Stirling Albion match and that time he was suspended for six weeks and it was made clear that 'a very serious view would be taken of any subsequent offence.' Strangely, Stirling Albion were again the opposition when the ultimate catastrophe came on August 28, 1954. Woodburn's capacity for becoming enraged during matches with such undistinguished opposition may be seen as confirmation of the obvious truth that his massive aberrations had little to do with an external context of events and were basically a manifestation of an internal problem, of the chemistry of his own personality. That is perhaps a facile interpretation, because there is no doubt that the pressures applied by the mere fact of being a Rangers player (a unique complication that will be considered in more detail later) are immensely relevant in any discussion of what happened to Woodburn.

It is questionable if many people, even among those who feel that they have a vivid recollection of Woodburn's removal from the game, can remember the man who was involved with him in the final sordid episode at Ibrox Park, the victim who, unintentionally, was the instrument of Woodburn's destruction as a footballer. He was Alec Paterson, the Stirling inside-left, a young man whose career before and after that brief, unfortunate period in the limelight was respectably obscure. The frightening simplicity of what happened on the field at Ibrox, the hideous suddenness of it and the sickening discrepancy between the trivial origins of the incident and the permanence of its implications – all this is conveyed in the cold, abbreviated account that emerged from the Referee Committee. 'When the game was almost finished Paterson, lying on the ground, caught Woodburn round the legs. As Paterson rose, Woodburn went towards him and struck him with his fist. When Woodburn was called he explained that he felt a jab of pain on his knee and lost his temper.' Woodburn's appearance before the Committee lasted exactly four minutes.

Naturally enough, there were few men in Scottish football who believed that the S.F.A. would adhere to the stunning terms of their judgment. Certainly Glasgow Rangers and their banished star were convinced that the Association would relent. Indeed, it was that confident expectation of a reprieve that prevented Woodburn from figuring in a remarkable court case, a challenge to football authority that would have been a highly controversial forerunner of George Eastham's successful action against Newcastle United. Woodburn had the ammunition to cause a furore in the courts but for several reasons – all of which can be seen in retrospect to have been inadequate – he decided against using it.

The man who armed him was John Cameron Q.C., now Lord Cameron, a Court of Session Judge. At the instruction of the Scottish Players' Union, Woodburn had sought an opinion from Cameron, probably the most impressive Scottish advocate of the day, and when it came it was explosive material. For thirty months after his suspension, Woodburn recalled later, the document lay in his desk 'like a smouldering fuse.' The opinion made it clear that if he went to law there was a real chance of having the verdict of the Referee Committee overturned. Cameron pointed out that the powers of suspending a player possessed by the S.F.A. were no-where clearly defined and that the *sine die* suspension really meant an indefinite and compulsory deprivation of the right to work or receive the reward. 'This is a very substantial power indeed,' wrote Cameron, 'and in my opinion not to be lightly inferred unless such a construction is in accordance with the natural meaning of the language used.' In considering Article 122 of the S.F.A. Cameron found the last sentence significant because it provided that a suspended player should be eligible to resume on the date on which his suspension expired. 'This is positively expressed,' insisted Cameron, 'and gives a right to the suspended player, a right to resume playing (and consequently earning money) from a pre-scribed and therefore presumably ascertainable date.' In any action the essence of Woodburn's argument would have been the fact that he had been suspended *sine die*, without definite date.

Cameron suggested that after a season the S.F.A. had no right to maintain the suspension, on the grounds that Woodburn's regis-tration lasted only until April 30 and that jurisdiction to suspend should only be exercisable in the case of registered players. He felt a *sine die* suspension was not warranted by the Articles of the S.F.A. In addition, he believed that the procedure followed at the hearings might have been such as to prevent the offender's case from being fairly presented or considered. Cameron concluded: 'I have only to add that I think the detailed circumstances of the hearing and occasion of the final suspension should be investigated in detail and also the circumstances of the ineffective appeal.'

Woodburn's reasons for declining to use these powerful words in a fight to get back into the game will appear peculiarly flimsy, even fatuous, to outsiders, but their influence must be related to his background and personal loyalties. For instance, he was heavily swayed by the comments of John Wilson, the elderly Glasgow bailie who was then chairman of Rangers. When he was shown the legal opinion and asked for his advice Bailie Wilson said: 'Don't take it as far as the courts. Rangers are behind you and we don't want to take it into court.' The desire to avoid that course if at all possible was shared by Woodburn. 'I had been a Rangers player for seventeen years and the club had been generous to me,' he wrote afterwards. 'The last thing I wanted to do was to bring it into open conflict with the S.F.A. and clearly if I had gone ahead Rangers would have been on my side. There was also the thought that if I won my fight against the S.F.A. and came back into football by means of a court order, things could be most awkward for me. I'd be a player apart, one who had challenged authority and won. Even if right was on my side I knew there would be people who would resent it . . . But most of all I was sure that after a reasonable period the ban would be lifted. I knew my offence merited a stiff punishment but when the sentence was pronounced words failed me completely. Later I thought of all the things I would have liked to have told the Referee Committee when asked if I had anything to say. I was still certain that after six months or even at the end of the 1954-55 season I would be cleared. I had given good service to Scotland. I was thirty-four and it was obvious that I didn't have many years left in football. The stigma of *sine die* was punishment enough. I had good grounds for believing that the S.F.A. might relent after a few months. There was the top legislator who had obviously heard that I was considering legal action. He phoned me with an urgent plea: 'Don't do it, Willie. Things will work out for the good, you'll see.'

'I was left with only one channel to get back into the game, to appeal to the S.F.A. – and even my appeals were rationed to one every six months.' When the second appeal was thrown out Woodburn's lawyers again pressed him to take his case into court but again he refused. 'I know one thing' he says now. 'If I was faced with the same decision today I wouldn't hesitate for a moment to carry my fight for justice to the limit.'

Eighteen months after the suspension the door was opened slightly when the S.F.A. ruled that Woodburn could come back into football – as anything except a player. Understandably, he saw that meagre concession as the equivalent of handing sweets to a child and warning him that he must not eat any. For him, re-enter-

WILLIE WOODBURN 'His use of the ball once he had won it was positive and accurate and his heading was prodigious, both in power and sureness of direction'

JOHN CHARLES 'Many sides have had to fear his skills, but none the misuse of his strength'

ing the game meant pulling on a pair of boots. But the total lifting
of the ban was not approved until April 23, 1957, and by then it
was too late. The inactivity had lasted just too long. Woodburn,
in the midst of his appealing and protesting and hoping, had become an ex-player. There was, he insists, substantial consolation in
the knowledge that a great deal of public sympathy was on his side.
Throughout the fight, players, fans and many officials had gone out
of their way to express their support. On the morning after he was
cleared he had two pleasant surprises. The first was a letter. It was
a benefit cheque from Rangers, £750 they had been unable to pay
him while he was under suspension. An hour later the doorbell
rang again and Woodburn found a telegram boy carrying a message
from his old rival, Gordon Smith, the great winger. The telegram
said: 'Hope to be playing against you soon.' Smith's brilliant
career, which had reached wonderful heights with Hibernian, was
to span exciting seasons with Hearts and Dundee but he was not to
be opposed by the formidable defensive skills of Woodburn again.

Inevitably, there were offers of jobs as a manager. Fulham invited Woodburn to take over at Craven Cottage and Bob Thyne,
a friend of long standing, asked him to fill the vacancy at
Kilmarnock. He declined with thanks. He has been doing the same
at intervals ever since. Apart from commentating on the game for
a newspaper and in occasional broadcasts, he has remained on the
outside. The fact that his name still has greater currency than that
of many a present-day player testifies to the scale of his achievements on the field. Admittedly, the dramatic nature of his
departure contributes to the longevity of the legend but its essence
is the relationship between the greatness of his career and the sadness of its ending. It was the distinction of the man involved that
made the sentence sensational, not the sentence that made the
player appear remarkable.

Even the background to Woodburn's arrival in football, and
later his arrival at Ibrox, was unusual. He was educated at George
Heriot's, a famous Edinburgh school whose boys were expected to
play rugby. For a long time he did spend his Saturday mornings in
the thick of the scrum and there can be little doubt that his strength,
athleticism and determination would have made him an extremely
successful rugby forward. But his heart was not in the game. He
was born so close to Tynecastle Park that as a boy he could watch
Hearts' home matches from his bedroom window and, naturally

G

enough, he became a rabid supporter. Alex Massie, Andy Anderson, J. A. ('Jean') Johnstone and Tommy Walker were among the dominant figures at Tynecastle in those days and loyalty to them precluded any possibility of more than a passing interest in Rangers. However, when Woodburn began playing centre-half for the juvenile team, Edinburgh Ashton, the sequence of events that was to take him to Ibrox was set in train. He resisted the appeals from Heriot's that he should go on playing rugby after leaving school at fifteen and devoted most of his leisure time to training and playing for Ashton. Reward came quickly.

In 1936 he played for the Scotland juvenile side against England at Leeds and after the match a Hearts scout, Jock White, gave him the thrilling news that his name would be mentioned favourably to the club. But, astonishingly, he heard nothing more from Hearts. An invitation to play trials with the Hampden Strollers XI, the Queen's Park reserve team, culminated in a similar disappointment. He had a few outings but no one asked him to sign and when he was demoted to the third team he went home convinced that he was not destined to be a footballer. Then a minor miracle happened. On October 6, 1937, he received a telegram that read: 'Can you play trial Ibrox Friday evening 6.30? Please phone – W. Struth.' He was so overwhelmed that when he made the call he forgot to reverse the charges and when he reached Ibrox the next evening he discovered that he had forgotten his boots. The Rangers trainer, Arthur Dixon, managed to find a pair of the right size (nine-and-a-half) that had been broken-in. In fact, the trainer's choice suggested an overdeveloped sense of symbolism. The boots he handed to the new boy belonged to Jimmy Simpson. Jimmy, the father of Ronnie Simpson, the goalkeeper in the fantastically successful Celtic team of recent seasons, is now a director of Rangers but in those days he was the first-team centre-half.

Woodburn was to step into his boots eventually but on that autumn evening in 1937 Arthur Dixon seemed disposed to anticipate the process. Despite giving away a penalty in that match against Third Lanark reserves, the 18-year-old trialist did sufficient to persuade Bill Struth to ask him to come up the marble staircase to the manager's office. The terms offered were £4 a week in the reserves and £8 plus bonuses in the first team. Almost too dazed to find the place for his signature on the forms, Woodburn accepted and walked out with a £20 signing-on fee and £2 expenses. It was not until he was on his way to catch the last train for Edinburgh that he remembered being warned before leaving home that he must not on any account sign a professional form. His father's main concern was that Willie should complete his apprenticeship as a plasterer so that he could go into the family business. But, looking back, the son is convinced that had Hearts been the club involved the father's objection would have been less strenuous. As it was, the confrontation was delayed, because the professional arrived home to find the rest of the family asleep and was able to sneak into bed. It was fortunate that he slept late because the morning newspaper was enough of a shock to Woodburn senior to put him off his breakfast. Not until his son had been established in the Rangers first eleven for some time did he admit grudgingly that perhaps it had been wise to accept Struth's offer. Willie still believes the old man may have been influenced by the fact that the automatic choice at centre-half for Scotland at the time was Jimmy Dykes – of Hearts.

Within a year of turning professional Woodburn was in the League side. There he learned quickly that fresh talent was not entirely welcomed by stars who saw their status threatened. He remembers that at that time the Rangers dressing-rooms operated on something like a players' prefect system. Any newcomer who was in danger of believing the eulogies of his friends found that the tongues of the older players provided a prompt, crude antidote. The conflict of generations was particularly tense at Ibrox when Woodburn was promoted because many of the men who had upheld Rangers' reputation through the thirties, outstanding players such as Bob McPhail, George Brown, Jimmy Simpson, Whitey McDonald, Bobby Main and Jimmy Smith were nearing the end of their careers and were being challenged by a group of highly promising recruits. A young centre-forward named Willie Thornton had been signed seven months before Woodburn and shortly afterwards, during the 1938 close-season, Rangers acquired a full-back, Jock Shaw, a left-half, Scot Symon, an inside-forward, Jimmy Duncanson, and an outside-right, Willie Waddell.

The standards set by the club in the decade before the Second World War can be gauged from their record against Arsenal between 1933 and 1938. In the annual meetings during that period – a golden passage in the history of Highbury – Rangers had three wins, two draws and only one defeat. Amid all the pressure of league and cup competitions, the friendly with Arsenal retained great significance for Rangers, and Woodburn and Thornton, already confirmed pals after travelling together on their regular journeys from the East of Scotland, were severely disappointed when their inexperience kept them out of the match at Ibrox on August 29, 1938. Woodburn had been looking forward to playing against Ted Drake. He was delighted, however, that the young contenders were to be represented by Waddell, who had been recognised as a prodigy since appearing for the reserves against Partick Thistle at the age of fifteen. Waddell and Thornton were to prove his closest friends during his seventeen years at Ibrox and it was natural that Woodburn should take pleasure in seeing the thrusting, wide-shouldered right-winger survive the attentions of Eddie Hapgood and score the only goal of the game. But the satisfaction was obviously increased by the knowledge that Waddell had given yet another warning that a new era was beginning at Ibrox. No one was to be more memorably indentified with the achievements of the next fifteen years or so than Woodburn, but first he had to withstand an appreciable setback.

Ironically, his troubles stemmed from Rangers' acquisition of George Young, a man Woodburn admires as much as any footballer who ever played with him. Young arrived as a spindly 19-year-old in September, 1941. He had been a left-back with Kirkintilloch Rob Roy and Woodburn, who had won a League Championship medal in his first season as a first-team player and was now in his third as Rangers' regular centre-half, was entitled to assume that this confident teenager was no threat to him. But before that month of September was out the whole situation had changed dramatically. The transformation was precipitated by a remarkable game at Easter Road. Rangers were labouring from the start against a Hibernian side that included two notable guests, Matt Busby and Bobby Baxter, and had Gordon Smith and Bobby Combe forming a damaging right wing. More relevant to Woodburn's personal predicament was the presence of Arthur Milne at centre-forward for Hibs. Milne was the small, elusive type of player that always gave him far more problems than the most powerful and aggressive of forwards. Milne, like the swift, darting Paddy Buckley of Aberdeen, was something of a jinx to Woodburn.

On that Saturday at Easter Road every Hibs man was a jinx to Rangers. The Glasgow team were 3-1 down before they really knew what was happening and when Woodburn moved upfield for a shot in an effort to stop the avalanche he ran into one of the worst moments of his career. His 30-yard drive was saved by Joe Crozier and when the goalkeeper punted the ball smartly towards the Rangers penalty area he had to scurry back to cover. He misjudged the flight of the ball and had to brake suddenly. There was no other player within yards but as he pulled up there was a sickening snap and his left knee buckled under him. After treatment he was able to struggle through the match, which degenerated into an 8-1 slaughter, with four goals from Bobby Combe, but the knee had swollen grotesquely by the finish and a cartilage operation was clearly unavoidable. By the time Woodburn reported fit three months later George Young was entrenched at centre-half.

It took Woodburn nearly five years to get back into the first eleven. During those years he played with the reserves in the North Eastern League. The competition offered a fairly high standard of football but when the Scottish League was re-formed after the war he found himself unwilling to accept anything short of the top level, so reluctantly he asked for a transfer. There were immediate approaches by Preston, Leicester and Arsenal but Woodburn, influenced by the persuasive arguments of Struth, delayed his decision and the problem solved itself when Dougie Gray, the longest serving player at Ibrox, decided to retire. Again George Young had a big effect on the situation. He moved to right-back and almost overnight Rangers had a defence whose strength, efficiency and assurance were intimidating. Scoring goals against them became so difficult that opponents who managed more than one goal were liable to feel they had had a triumphant afternoon.

Apart from Waddell and Thornton, the Rangers attack of the period was inclined to be moderate but its deficiencies were far outweighed by the quality of the defence. Time and again a match was won by scoring one goal (more often than not through a Waddell centre and a Thornton header) and resolutely shutting out the opposition for the rest of the hour-and-a-half. It was not an approach calculated to put the neutral spectator in ecstasies but the vast Rangers support, for whom the first criterion has always been success, were not likely to complain. The cups and championships were collected with a remorseless regularity that almost suggested the working of a natural law and, in addition to the satisfaction of tangible achievement the committed thousands on the terraces could point to the deep, slow-pulsing excitement to be had from watching formidable men imposing their talents and their collective will upon events. Football teams whose most dramatic names, most stirring personalities, are in defence are rare but, while again acknowledging the excellence of Waddell and Thornton, that can be said of the Rangers of those days. The side owed its ethos and its style as well as most of its success to the six men in the positions from goal to left-half. In trying to find a vivid shorthand description of this phenomenon, this unique defence, the sportswriters of the immediate post-war years could be forgiven for borrowing from Churchill. The Iron Curtain, they called it, and few of the forwards of other clubs in the Scottish First Division considered the implied praise excessive.

The first member of that defence was not entirely typical. Bobby Brown, the present manager of the Scotland team, was a blond, handsome, acrobatically graceful goalkeeper. He had come from Queen's Park and he never quite lost that vague air of refinement that tradition associates (in defiance of much of the factual evidence) with the outstanding amateur. In front of Brown there were no such hints of Corinthian gentility. The men who strove to keep the ball away from him were uncompromising professionals and they were not too concerned if they had to receive or inflict a few bruises to prove it. George Young, with his bizarre physique (a huge, high-shouldered torso on long, seemingly elastic legs) was a defender with a range of natural attributes and cultivated skills that eventually gave him far more international caps than any other Scottish player in history. He captained his country eight times against England alone.

The style of play favoured by Jock Shaw at left-back could almost be deduced from the severity of his haircut and the ferocity of his soubriquet, Tiger. Tenacity was the essence of his game and wingers did not find his company restful on Saturday afternoons. At right-half was Ian McColl, another who subsequently had experience of managing the Scotland team. McColl was a strong, intelligent, free-striding wing-half who could kill the ball with stunning facility regardless of how it came to him. Only a tendency to pass inaccurately prevented him from being a really great player.

There was simply no question about the greatness of Sammy Cox, whether he was playing left-half, as he generally did when part of the Iron Curtain, or left-back, as he did with remarkable success when required for Scotland and Rangers. Cox, a stocky, resilient Ayrshireman, was a magnificent tackler and he passed firmly and precisely, striking the ball with thrilling crispness with either foot. He read the play perceptively and he was quite fearless. Many good judges in Scotland will tell you that Cox was as fine a defensive half-back as ever played in British football. At least as many will tell you that he was the most distinguished member of that tremendous Rangers defence. Those who disagree will probably split just about evenly into advocates of Young and advocates of Woodburn. My own feeling is that Cox and Woodburn had slightly more irrefutable class than Young, though his inspiring presence and wonderful temperament ensured that neither of the others was likely to be a more significant influence on any game than he was. What is certain is that no one, not Cullis nor Ocwirk or Santamaria nor even John Charles, ever looked the part of the great centre-half more than Woodburn. These are players he admired hugely – along with Neil Franklin – and it can be taken that all five reciprocated the respect.

Woodburn's slimness and his upright bearing made the unmistakable strength of his body all the more impressive. When a man stands over six feet and has substantial bulk he has to be utterly exceptional – to be a John Charles in fact – to avoid an impression of grossness on the football field. Woodburn, lean and hard and big only where it really mattered, exuded athletic vigour. But he was the least hectic of players. He had a purposeful, economical stride and in the main he used it to patrol a flexible crescent beyond the edge of the penalty area, vigilant for incipient trouble through the middle or from the flanks. Essentially he covered a zone rather than an individual opponent and was drawn to the wings only when he was sure his intervention would be profitable. 'There was no point in going out there to fanny about,' he says in his slightly lilting Edinburgh accent. 'If you went you had to make up your mind that you were going to get the ball.' Woodburn's tackling, its strength multiplied by superb timing, made it difficult for the best of forwards to prevent him from getting the ball. He employed one foot as decisively as the other and one of his most spectacular assets was the ability to run alongside a forward who was breaking clear and time the sliding tackle so precisely that he not only dispossessed the opponent but pushed the ball to a fellow defender, all in one movement. His use of the ball once he had won it was positive and accurate and his heading was prodigious, both in power and sureness of direction.

Basically he could play any type of forward but, as I indicated earlier, the small, tricky players had more hope of disconcerting him than had the muscular hustlers. He relished meeting such powerful, physically aggressive attackers as Trevor Ford, Tommy Lawton, Jackie Milburn and Stan Mortensen, and gave some of his best performances against them. 'There was never any squealing from those fellows,' he says in explanation of his preference. 'They gave it and took it and got on with the game.' The essence of Woodburn's greatness in his prime was his consistency, the class that was inseparable from his play every time he took the field. That is as it should be with defenders and it is scarcely meaningful to recall particular matches. However, understandably, he remembers with special pleasure his three appearances against England at Wembley in 1947, 1949 and 1951, because none was on a losing side. In the first of the matches he was in a team that had been reckoned to have slightly less chance than the Light Brigade at Balaclava. He played outstandingly well in curbing Lawton and Scotland took a deserved 1-1 draw. In the 1949 victory he was leading member of the supporting cast on an occasion that belonged to Jimmy Cowan, who gave a display of defiant goalkeeping that was almost laughable in its extravagant brilliance, and in 1951 he did much to help the Scots exploit the misfortune that diminished a courageous England side when Mannion went off injured after only quarter of an hour.

Altogether Woodburn was capped five times against England, four times against Wales, four times against Ireland, three times against France, twice against Belgium, twice against Austria and once against Portugal, Denmark and America. His international record, which also included seven appearances in inter-League matches, must be seen in the light of the extreme eccentricity that traditionally afflicts Scottish selectors. In most other countries Woodburn would have been an immovable feature of the national team. The Scots, typically, felt entitled to lift or leave his great talent. However few of those who played with him or against him had any doubts about his worth.

None had a better opportunity to judge him on and off the field than Willie Waddell, who shared so much of his Rangers and Scotland careers. Waddell, a determined, engagingly forthright man, whose achievements as a manager with Kilmarnock brought five-figure offers from England before he chose to be a full-time journalist, is unequivocal: 'Willie Woodburn impressed me more as a footballer and a man than anyone else I have ever met in the game. As a centre-half he had everything. That is said about a lot of players but with him it was literally true. The thing that always struck me most about him was that he had no weak side. It didn't matter whether the ball was coming at him from the left or the right, in the air or on the ground, he took it with the same perfect timing, the same tremendous authority. Only the really great defenders can do that. The fact is that you couldn't think of a quality you would want in a man in that position that Woodburn didn't have – unless, of course, you included a balanced temperament. Willie would admit – well, he'd have no option, would he? – that he had deficiencies in that respect. But it would be absolutely ridiculous to think of him as a maliciously violent man. You couldn't meet a more generous, likeable man. Tell me how many people in the game really disliked him.

'Some of the wild men in football come from rough backgrounds where they had to fight or be trampled underfoot. But Willie comes from a marvellous family, quite well-off and terrifically respectable. They were always a very united family, very close, just as Willie is with his wife and three daughters. He was brought up to behave like a gentleman and if he didn't always manage it on the field there were very special reasons for that. He was always a fierce competitor, a real professional who considered it his job to go out there and give everything he had. But I think that basic determination was distorted by the mystique of Rangers. There is no doubt that in our time the very act of pulling that blue jersey over your head did something to you. All the talk about tradition, about the privilege and responsibility that went with being a Rangers player, definitely had its effect. Obviously, a lot of it was nonsense, a mixture of myths and exaggerations that put things completely out of perspective, but it got through to us as players. The atmosphere of Ibrox, the attitude of everyone connected with the club, made you feel that it was your duty to shatter all opposition, to prove that there was only one Rangers. I remember we had a fellow playing with us called Eddie Rutherford. Eddie was the nicest character you could meet, the nicest man in the team. He was always smiling. But when we lost I used to hate him. "Look at that wee bastard,' I used to say. 'He's still smiling.' It was crazy, I suppose, but that's how we felt and I think Woodburn felt it more than any of us. I am sure that obsession with winning for Rangers had a lot to do with his troubles.'

Woodburn's nickname among his team mates was Big Ben, which might be interpreted as a tribute to his size and total reliability. In fact, he earned the name in Lisbon in the late forties after Rangers had trounced Benfica. At the celebration afterwards Woodburn insisted on raising his glass every few minutes and bellowing 'Viva Benfica.' He went on doing it well into the next day and Waddell and a few others felt his performance had to be permanently commemorated. Waddell was unlikely to forget that trip in any case. He was immediately attracted to the hostess on the plane going out and she was soon his wife. 'The last time we met Woodburn he picked up the wife and nearly broke half-a-dozen ribs.' Waddell told me. She said, 'That man's mad.' I said 'Well you've known him long enough now.' He can be wild. Yet when I was best man at his wedding I had to hold his hand all through the ceremony.'

Sheer vitality, an immense physical vigour that is constantly threatening to spill over into horseplay, is one of the first characteristics one notices in Woodburn. After a few drinks at a party he is liable to deliver some friendly shoulder charges or lift someone off his feet just for fun. The only occasions when I have seen his good nature clouded with resentment have all been associated with football. Apart from owning a garage and being a partner in the family building business, he does journalistic work and when he is in the Press box he plays every ball, kicking the boards in front of his legs, leaping from his seat as a player strains for a header. At the end of a recent under-23 international in which the England team gave Scotland some harsh treatment, he strode along behind the rows of English reporters, saying in a loud, challenging voice: 'Hammer throwers, bloody hammer throwers.'

Fortunately, no one was unwise enough to question the judgment. I agree with Willie Waddell's assessment of Woodburn's generosity of nature and I, too, like him a great deal. But there is a deep reservoir of violence in the man and anyone who opens the sluice gates had better be a strong swimmer. There is no point in wailing over that explosive temper. It is part of him. We should be grateful that before it did its ultimate damage we had a good long look at one of the greatest centre-halves who ever kicked a ball.

SIX

John Charles

by Tony Pawson

THERE WAS a sad nostalgic paragraph tucked away in the corner of the Sports Page of the evening paper: —
'John Charles is back on the warpath. The 35-year-old former Welsh International centre-forward struck brilliant form in recent league matches. He is really in the groove playing some great stuff. He could win the tie for us single-handed if he could stay in this mood, said Hereford manager Bob Dennison.'

Here was one of the great players of all time and of all countries in the twilight of his career. And it was typical that his love for the game should lead him to prefer the obscurity of the Southern League to the inactivity of the stand. A few years ago John Charles' form was headline material, not a fill-in piece to make up the page. Then the matches he was likely to win single-handed were for Wales, or Juventus, or Leeds. It is sad to think of that great talent no longer in the limelight of soccer's showpieces. But is it tragedy or triumph that 'King' Charles who once held Italy's extravagant football world in awe should fade from the soccer scene in a humble and penurious League? Inevitably there is regret that he should not have taken his farewells at the height of his powers and reputation. There is sadness too that so versatile a player should have failed to stay at the top in his early thirties. Many a soccer player matures to his best at this age.

Leslie Compton was thirty-nine when he won his first International Cap for England. Another centre-half, Jack Charlton, was the outstanding defender in the outstanding defence that won England the World Cup in 1966. And Jack Charlton then was over thirty and is still likely to be with the England team in Mexico in 1970. When Wales met Hungary in the World Cup in Sweden another former centre-forward, Hideguti, was Charles' opposite number and he was already thirty-six. Those unique wingers, the Welshman Billy Meredith and the incomparable Sir Stanley Matthews, have shown that it is possible to retain the skills and the fitness to be playing First Division football on the verge of fifty. They are the exceptions which prove no rule, for both were laws to themselves. But many more mundane players have held their place in top class soccer at John Charles' age and it is sad that his unusual gifts are no longer on view to the great crowds.

Yet sadness takes second place to admiration. It is typical of

Charles that his love of the game keeps him playing no matter what the level. It is typical of his modesty and his quiet composure that, after lording it over Wales and Italy, he can play for Hereford with no loss of pride or enjoyment. Here at once is illuminated one side of his greatness. He had the most powerful physique of any of his generation of footballers and few have been harrassed or provoked as he was. Those who wanted to win at any price and those who found genius intolerably humiliating and irritating were only too keen to hack him down to their size. Yet he never lost his temper, never retaliated, never made unfair use of his weight and strength. Never sent off, never booked or cautioned, he was the model of good sportsmanship throughout his first-class career and he is still playing with the same unblemished approach.

Many sides have had to fear his skills, but none the misuse of his strength. The only time he was observably angry and belligerent in his play was when his brother Mel had been injured by an outrageous tackle in a game against Austria. Mel was carried off the field on a stretcher fourteen minutes from the end of a match that remains a by-word for roughness. John Charles, already injured himself, at last lost his habitual poise and took his full share in the battle that left the dressing-rooms looking like casualty clearing stations. It was characteristic of a man whose heart is as big as his body that he should be unselfish even in anger. For himself he took in his calm stride all that was flung at him in the direct physical clash of English football, or the sly exasperating obstruction of the Italian League with its occasional outbursts of Latin temperament.

Today there is endless emphasis on so-called soccer violence. In fact the new violence is on the terraces, rather than the field of play. Standards of fitness are higher and to that extent the game is harder and faster than it used to be. But it is no rougher than before. Only memory wraps the past in a warm glow selectively retaining the best and rejecting the worst. Even the great modern flare-ups like Celtic v. Racing Club of Argentine had their equivalents in the 'Battle of Highbury' between England and Italy in 1934, or the World Cup 'Battles of Bordeaux and Berne' with Brazil figuring prominently in these two disgraceful conflicts of 1938 and 1954. High stakes and a clash of styles and temperaments have always been explosive material on the soccer field. From time to time spirit takes control of sense in any era and any season.

In his career in top-class soccer John Charles had to take as much and more of a battering than most current players. Always he absorbed the punishment with unruffled dignity and without hint of irritation. No wonder he won the title 'the Gentle Giant.'

All great players whatever their sport are almost by definition men or women of outstanding character, people with personal qualities that distinguish them from the crowd. Soccer's great seem to be of three distinct types. Those like Denis Law or Norbert Stiles or Hans Beckenbauer have a flair and an explosive enthusiasm that drives them beyond the disciplined competence of their fellows. Then there are the peacock showmen like Len Shackleton or John Charles' Juventus clubmate, Sivori, who must always display and sometimes waste their skills in extravagant and flamboyant exhibition of their superior talent. Finally there are the natural 'gentlemen', the quiet self-effacing imperturbable men who let genius speak for itself. There was never any doubt that this was John Charles' category, along with Stanley Matthews, Tom Finney, Billy Wright, Lev Yashin, or Eusebio Ferreira.

This is greatness shared, but in one quality Charles stands alone in football's scrolls of fame. He has the frame of a rugby forward and yet he achieved the delicacy of touch, the certainty of balance and the quickness in turning that could match any small elusive player. During his career he has been left-half, right-back, centre-half, inside-forward and centre-forward. And he was equally at home in any position. It is unique for someone so big of build to be so versatile and to rely so little on his physical power. Had he been less of a gentleman and with more of the killer instinct he might have been even more effective on the field. He could easily have emulated Monti, the man who won so many games for Argentine and Italy by uninhibited use of his strength. Yet John Charles' approach made him not only the better sportsman, but the better all round player who was not confined to the centre of the field.

Aptly enough, for soccer success 'S' is the magic letter. Skill, speed, subtlety, sensitivity, spirit and strength are the essential qualities that bring a team or an individual to the top. In this list of priorities strength is a bad last for if rugby is a man's game, soccer is an intelligent man's game with the emphasis on cleverness and control. John Charles, six-feet-two in height and fourteen stone in weight, was hardly designed by nature for a game that relies on quickness of reaction and sureness of touch. Yet he has proved that even in association football the good big-'un may be better than the good little-'un. And he has proved it without ever using his strength to subvert the rules, or crush his opponent's spirit. From time to time he received the inevitable advice on how to deal with a tricky player who was getting the better of him. It was nicely wrapped up, of course, but the message was clear 'Use your weight, John. After a few shoulder charges and a strong tackle or two he will stop all this nonsense.' It was rare for a player of Charles' size to need the advice, unique for him to ignore it and rely on his own skills.

For me there is one scene that sums up John Charles' great qualities of character and soccer skill, the way that his presence alone could frighten opponents into defeat. It was at the Solna Stadium at Stockholm in 1958 as Wales played off against Hungary for a place in the quarter-finals of the World Cup. The background was hardly propitious for a stirring match. Wales had been fortunate to qualify for the finals in Sweden. Hungary, no longer the dominating force in World soccer, were still a powerful team. True Wales had held them to a 1–1 draw in their first meeting, but they had been saved only by a great header from John Charles as he soared to meet a corner with the desperate defenders bouncing helplessly off his chest. And this had been followed by a dreary draw against the incompetent Mexicans. Another draw had followed by kind permission of the Swedes, who were already certain to head their group and took a tactical rest, playing five reserves and not bothering about goals. Even so, it had needed some inspired goalkeeping by Jack Kelsey and some incredible misses by 'Nacka' Skoglund whose clowning usually had a more effective and deadly conclusion.

There had been the usual wrangle with the Italian Football Federation before John Charles was released for the World Cup and he had not yet fitted happily into the side. His presence too seemed to awe his colleagues as much as his opponents so that he received a sorry service. Even great players like Ivor Allchurch appeared to shrink in stature as if so dwarfed by him, mentally and physically, that they mistrusted their own powers. So they had let play flow round him like minor executives hurrying about their own business and avoiding contact with their formidable Managing Director. The setting and the start did nothing to alleviate the depression. England were playing Russia in Gothenburg and attention was centred there. The Solna Stadium was sadly empty, except for a handful of Swedes and a group of Hungarians whose thoughts were as much on politics as on soccer. Imre Nagy, leader of the Hungarian Insurrection against their Russian masters, had been executed twenty-four hours earlier. Now at a sporting occasion to promote goodwill among men, Free Hungarians draped in black made their protest at man's inhumanity to man. Reluctantly and kindly many of them were shepherded away by the police. To add to irony of the situation, the referee was a Russian, Latychev, and judged by his performance he may well have felt it was not a day for him to be hard on the Hungarians. So there was to be no protection from him for John Charles who was the sole target of Hungary's tactical plans. Despicable as this might be for a country who had so recently led the World, they had a clear plan to shackle Charles by whatever means. There could have been no greater tribute to a player than that these masters of soccer should rate him so highly that they were prepared to do anything, however illegal, to stop him.

In the earlier meeting, on a clear sunny evening in the little stadium of Sandviken, not far from the Arctic Circle, Charles soon found how frightened the Hungarians were of him. Three times in a painful first sixteen minutes he was hacked down, once by right-winger Karoly Sandor coming back to catch him from behind. By then Wales were a goal down as Jack Kelsey for once was deceived by a shot from Bozsik that came low out of the shadow of the stand into the blazing sunlight. Yet despite the vicious treatment John Charles inspired Wales to fight back and himself snatched the equaliser despite all the elbowing and holding. This confirmed the Hungarian estimate and Hungarian fears. So for the play-off at Solna Charles was marked for destruction as Pele was to be in later World Cups. Whenever there was a corner one player pinned his arms while another smashed into him from behind. The referee smiled benignly and let play go on. At the Press Conference afterwards he explained that he had been playing the advantage rule. Correspondents were too astounded to ask whose advantage he was concerned with. Certainly not Charles's and certainly he gave no protection to a man who never retaliated.

Soon Wales were a goal down as Budai burst away and Tichy drove home the centre. Before half-time too Charles was crippled.

The same Hungarian player smashed him down yet again and for a time he had to leave the field. But soon he hobbled back to float over the perfect centre. Eager as a whippet Ivor Allchurch streaked

H

in on the ball, swung his left leg and smashed the volley into the net wide of Grosics. With Bowen controlling them and driving them on, a magnificent captain drawing a splendid response, the whole team fought with a fine dispassionate fury. There was a cold determination to outplay the Hungarians by skill and spirit. The crippled Charles was their talisman and suddenly it was a team of Charleses playing with perfect sportsmanship and deadly determination against the wild and desperate Hungarians. Sixteen minutes from time Medwin slipped away on his own, sped past Saroso and flicked the ball home. It was a famous victory, ending the legend of the magical Magyars. From drab beginnings and dreary opposition the Welsh fashioned a match as dramatic and thrilling as any I have seen. While John Charles focussed the attention and drained the resources of the Hungarians the other red shirts surged through to victory. This was the glory of Wales and if their triumph was short-lived, their departure from the competition was no less honourable.

A few days later Wales had to face the brilliant Brazilians with John Charles still too badly injured to take part. They were defeated by a solitary goal from a little known youngster of seventeen, Pele. That was the greatest achievement of Welsh football, the best performance of any British team in the World Cup until England won it at Wembley. If John Charles had been fit would the established master have gone one better than the star to be? Might Wales have beaten the two great teams of Europe and South America in successive matches? Fascinating speculation, but only one thing is certain. It was the final confirmation of Charles' calibre that the question should be seriously asked. It is now soccer's supreme accolade for the famous that they should be regarded as too dangerous to be allowed to survive a World Cup series. Among the many precedents he set it was his involuntary, and least happy achievement to become the first of these marked men, the target of planners who saw him as a formidable obstacle blocking their path to the Jules Rimet Cup. This is a tawdry development in a great competition, but it is a small and select group who have been eminent enough to merit this individual attention.

It was as a goal-scoring centre-forward that Charles was most feared, but as a centre-half he played some of his finest games for Wales. Two Internationals in the 1955/56 season best illustrated his powers for combining impregnable defence with a readiness to thrust swiftly into attack. That was the season the Welsh might so easily have won the home International championship. They began with their first victory over England for seventeen years. In the charged atmosphere of Ninian Park it was Charles who held off the early English assaults. Finney and Matthews cut through continually as if Cardiff had bestowed on them the freedom of the wing. But it was wasted brilliance, for John Charles was dominating the centre, sealing off every opening with his usual massive calm. Steadily he reversed the tide of play, bringing his forwards into the game until England suddenly and surprisingly cracked under the mounting pressure. Just before half-time Tapscott raced through unchallenged to take Kinsey's pass and sweep the ball beyond Williams' reach. A minute later Cliff Jones had put Wales two up with a characteristic flying header. For once Charles misapplied his attacking skills heading home with fine certainty – past his own goalkeeper, Jack Kelsey. It was a momentary aberration that never ruffled his cool control of the English forwards who remained unusually subdued.

A win against Ireland would have ensured the Championship for Wales and John Charles set it up for them with one brilliant thrust. Breaking from his own area he ran the length of the field, as defender after defender failed to check his irresistible momentum. On the edge of the Irish area he crossed a pass that Ford stepped over and Clarke hit home. But this was a day when genius was to cancel out genius. Danny Blanchflower was the Irish captain and it was his tactical skill and penetrating passes that finally ripped open the Welsh defence. Time after time he sent Bingham darting behind Hopkins and not even John Charles could cut out every pass. So it was that Jimmy Jones scored the equalising goal. To look at, Jones was a caricature of a centre-forward, balding, overweight, and with his shorts too small. But there was no humiliation for Charles that Jones should score against him. The only wonder was that the lancing attacks of Bingham and Blanchflower brought no spate of goals. There was no doubt about the verdict of Charles' play. As one writer put it 'But when we review the game now and in the future this summary is inevitable – the John Charles match.'

As unquestionable is Charles' place in soccer history now and in the future. But what were the special attributes of his play that singled him out as Europe's leading footballer? Inevitably a part of his success was intelligent use of his great physique. First he had to overcome the crippling disadvantages that usually handicap the outsize player. Normally he will be slow and clumsy lacking in delicate control. No advantage of height or strength can offset these defects. But John Charles trained himself to have the speed, the balance, the quickness of reaction that made him the equal of any quick-silver forward. Admittedly he was more at home in the leisured pace of Italian football than in the rush and hustle of the English game. Admittedly he was more favoured by the Continental techniques of screening the ball, where he was encouraged to use his bulk to baulk the attacker. Yet he held his own against the push and run tactics favoured in English football and in the face of the 'make it simple, make it quick' philosophy that put a premium on speed and directness. And once he could match anyone at this style of play then, for the rest, his size was sheer bonus. In the penalty area his height and weight made him a commanding figure whether in attack or defence. A high ball was his ball and no-one could stop him getting it. Many of his goals were irresistible headers as he climbed above everyone else. There was no more fascinating duel than to watch Billy Wright trying to match the big man in the air. It was not as unequal a contest as mere size indicated. As if he suffered from a surfeit of sympathy for others, Charles rarely seemed at his best against a small opponent. Wright, too, had both the courage and the natural spring that enabled him to make a formidable challenge. Yet Charles was one of the few he never mastered.

The other advantage that size gave John Charles as a defender was solidity in the tackle. No forward could force his way past Charles and those who tried jarred to a halt. Conversely, his weight gave him a formidable power as an attacker, a terrible man to tame. It was an exhilarating sight to see Charles going for the ball with the momentum of a runaway tank. Once launched to strike, no-one could hold him. Had he not been so scrupulously fair, so careful how he used his weight, he would have been a real danger to limbs as well as to the goal. In the normal skills of the game he was a British player who was in advance of his time. Sir Alf Ramsey won the World Cup for England by dispensing with specialists and fixed positions and relying on players who were mobile in thought and action. It was essential that all had the full range of skills and a fluid approach that meant an easy switch from attack to defence. This was the lesson that Charles absorbed early.

Having been a back, a wing-half, and a forward, playing now on the left, now on the right, now in the centre, he could understand and anticipate the trend of play over the whole field. Again, he was almost the first to appreciate that Continental football had much to teach us. He was a natural target for the business acumen of Agnelli and the acute perception of Peronaci as these two tried to attract the world's best talent to Juventus. But he was not just bought by money – tempting though the bait was. He was attracted by the challenge of Italian football and had the sense to set out to enjoy it and to adapt to it. In doing so he learnt a different approach, a different emphasis to British players. He improved his ball control and his mastery of the close passing game. More important, he appreciated that quick thinking is as vital as quick moving. He was one of the first to initiate the quiet revolution that has transformed British soccer.

While it is still fashionable to praise the past it is, in fact, quite clear that in the last decade there has been a startling rise in the standard of ball-play common in First Division football. One takes it for granted now that the players are masters of the basic skills and it was this that we learnt from the Continentals. Run, run, run may still be the basis of British football, but it is backed by instinctive control. The World Cup was won because the players relied not solely on speed and fitness, but first on matching their opponents' skills then on raising the pace to add a new dimension. The priorities were right again and our position in World soccer restored. John Charles was one of the few who maintained our prestige in the lean years of the fifties and helped to set us back on the right course. In August 1955 the United Kingdom was defeated 4–1 by the Rest of Europe and it was a depressing revelation of their superior arts. Only three of our players were their equals in ball control and in subtlety. John Charles, together with the ageless Stanley Matthews and Danny Blanchflower, alone preserved our pride and pointed the way to better things.

Charles' potential was quick to show. As a youngster of twelve he was in the Swansea schoolboys team helping them to the quarter-final of the English Schools Trophy Competition. But he was not yet big of body or reputation. When he joined Swansea Town in 1946 he was fourteen years old and described by Roy Paul as a 'slip of a boy.' But it was not long before he attracted the attention of the scouts for his natural gift for soccer was never dependent on his size. He was approached by Alf Pickard and offered terms with Leeds United. His father, himself a talented amateur player, judged the opportunity too good to miss. Young Charles took his advice and it may well have been better than he knew. For Leeds United had a manager who was unusually perceptive and progressive. Major Buckley had made his name with Wolverhampton Wanderers where his drive for fitness had brought a blaze of publicity over his monkey gland treatment. But if that was something of a gimmick he had other more valuable ideas that attracted less attention. One of his coaching concepts was to make every player equally competent with either foot and ready to play in any position. So the apprehensive youngster who had been playing left-half found himself down as a right-back for his first practice game with Leeds.

If Major Buckley was prepared to give his players the occasional psychological shock, there was always a sound reason for it. When it came to blooding his youngsters in the first team he planned their induction with the same care that Matt Busby has always shown. John Charles was seventeen when his chance came. But it was a game without strain or tension. For it was the final match of the season and it was away from home against Blackburn Rovers. When it mattered the youngster was given the opportunity to establish himself quietly and to gain his confidence far from the critical eyes of the home crowd. Buckley, who discovered so many fine players was taking care to launch his 'greatest find' in a way that would command success.

Charles had filled out now and, as he gained in power, he soon caught the eye of the Welsh selectors. What a contrast and what a lesson in their inept handling of a promising prospect compared with Buckley's meticulous planning. There was to be no easy and tactful introduction for Charles. In the next season, before he had any real experience of League football behind him, he was chosen to play against Ireland at Wrexham. Worse, he was given the type of press build-up that he could barely have justified at the height of his maturity and greatness. Prodigy he might be, but this was too much for his nerves to stand. The Irish centre-forward, Dave Walsh of Aston Villa, was an old campaigner cool and clever enough to take fair advantage. Playing relentlessly on Charles' inexperience and his apprehension, he tormented him with every trick and twist of the trade. Desperate covering and frantic tackling closed the gaps behind Charles as he was left stranded and despondent. So

Wales survived and the game was a goalless draw. But great expectations had invited great disappointment and the criticism was merciless. The prodigy was written off as a failure and it was not until 1951 that he was given another trial.

Then, with the same lack of feeling, he was brought back to the scene of his disaster, picked to play at Wrexham again against the Swiss. To add to his problems, this was a strong team with a novel method in which wing-halves marked the wingers, the left-back covered the centre, while centre-forward and centre-half mastered the mid-field. So he found it difficult to come to grips with the elusive Bickel, the first deep-lying centre-forward he had met. Fortunately Wales stormed to a 3–0 lead, but once they came under pressure themselves, Charles and his colleagues were soon struggling. So a triumphal progress turned into a desperate rearguard action as Wales held on grimly to win 3–2.

It was another two years before Charles was able to establish himself, but by then he was a confident and versatile player sure of his own strength and skills. This time there was no faltering as he lashed in one goal with a left-foot volley, took another with a superb header, then made the opening for a third. So Ireland were beaten 3–2 and Charles, playing at inside, was both planner and spearhead of victory. This was the first successful pairing of two formidable strikers. With Trevor Ford he formed as dangerous a spearhead as the game could offer. Even when he had to put up with four positional changes in six matches for Wales his poise was unassailable. Once more he had the astute Major Buckley to thank for the transformation. For it was Buckley who suddenly switched him to centre-forward in what the papers characterised as an emergency move. But it was a planned gamble for Leeds, and it brought the best out of Charles. From the start he began to get goals and the temporary trial was soon a permanent arrangement. In his first season as centre-forward he scored more than thirty goals and followed it up with forty-two out of the Leeds tally for the season of eighty-nine. It was not long before Leeds achieved their promotion to the First Division managed now by Raich Carter with his silver hair and silver tongue.

Charles now was one of soccer's chosen and his golden touch had a glitter that soon attracted the game's most acquisitive buyers. In Italy soccer had become the sport of millionaires and money was no object in the battle for prestige. Juventus, struggling near the bottom of the League, were backed by the wealth of Signor Agnelli and the determination to rise to the top. The voluble and perceptive Gigi Peronace chose Charles as the player most likely to help them. Perhaps it was an obvious choice, but it was a happy one. Out of the World's best there was no better for their purpose. So the bargaining began with the shadow of relegation hanging over Juventus and the knowledge that the deal would never go through if they slipped to the Second Division, in which no foreigners were allowed. Leeds recognised that the financial rewards were too great for Charles to scorn and gave every help to him and his financial adviser in concluding the deal. This was a welcome change of attitude from the earlier xenophobia of the League Managements. Understandable fears that we would lose some of our best players had turned to obsessive and irrational opposition to any overseas transfers. Every obstacle had been put in the way of such deals and ostracism was the lot of those, like Neil Franklin, who ignored them. At last there was a more liberal approach, recognising that we could not indefinitely deny our players the lucrative offers from countries like Italy while maintaining our own tight and limited pay structure with its maximum wage and rigid control of transfer fees. This was reluctant acceptance of the inevitable, rather than a recognition of the advantages. For there were advantages. As some of the great British players began to move abroad the constricting isolationism of British soccer was broken at last. Not only did the individual footballers like John Charles, or Denis Law, or Jimmy Greaves, learn new methods and communicate them back home, but by playing abroad they focussed attention on developments in standards and styles overseas. At last there was an overdue interest in the main stream of soccer ideas, rather than the narrow introvert concentration on our own game. It was not the countries like Italy and Spain who bought in the World's best who gained. Instead they found their own standards declining. Their home players were overshadowed and dwarfed, while the countries from whom they attracted the talent were stimulated by having new targets to achieve, fresh ideas to consider. John Charles was the man who set the fashion. Others had gone before, like Paddy Sloan and Eddie Firmani, but it was Charles' great reputation and greater success that made the trend respectable.

At once Charles was at home with Juventus. He liked the country and the people, and the style of play suited his special abilities.

Eddie Firmani had already recorded how the close defensive game heightened his own skills. 'I realised the true significance of close marking and how a footballer – great though he might be as a ball player or a sharp shooter – could never hope for success unless he 'escaped' from those given the job of marking him. I started to move away from defenders and into any open space I found available. Because of the close support of my colleagues I was able to find my way to goal.' Firmani was soon scoring regularly despite the defensive 'bolt' system that was so difficult to penetrate. John Charles found the same problem, the same opportunities 'I discovered that football is not played with players moving away from each other. It is played with players moving into spaces, moving close to the man with the ball. And it is not played at breakneck speed all the time.'

What a change from English League football with its emphasis, at the time, on the long ball and direct running with few subtle changes of pace or direction. There was a change too in the type of tackling. It was customary at the time to find fault with Italian football on the basis of condemning what one did not understand. So it was soon being widely publicised that Charles had said 'In Italian soccer when they tackle, they tackle to kill.' In fact he had made no such quote and was too intelligent to ignore the evidence of fewer injuries than in the British game. Physical contact took second place to positional play, to screening the ball with the body, to winning it by clever interception. There was less direct challenge, more obstruction and jostling; less manly confrontation, more sly sophistication and childish outbursts. The slower pace suited Charles and his individual strength and skill allowed him to dominate even a packed penalty area. He had the power to win any loose ball, the bulk to screen it successfully as he held off every challenge. Yet Juventus had bought more than a big man with a gift for soccer. Charles' massive calm, his dignified poise was a stabilising influence in the tense emotional atmosphere of the Italian League. He was as impervious to the temperament of opponents as to the adulation or invective of the crowds. Under his influence Juventus became relaxed and confident enough to soar to the top. Three times they became League Champions; twice they won the Cup. Inevitably they paid grateful homage to 'King' Charles for leading them to their goals.

Italian tactics were based on protection for the goalkeeper with only two strikers upfield and eight players thinking first in terms of defence. Possession of the ball was nine-tenths of the law with all players expert in close control and close passing. This ability to beat a man meant that there was little midfield challenge. Delay and retreat was the order of the day until the defensive cover was solid, the penalty area too packed to penetrate. It was a style that made goals a rarity and the spectators had to get their enjoyment in part from the results, in part from the skills. Two types of player attracted their fancy, won their applause. There was the spectacular mid-field exhibitionist, a ball juggler like Sivori, Charles' even more expensive colleague. Often Sivori was so intoxicated with his own cleverness that he would waste the opening made by putting his foot on the ball and acknowledging the applause of the crowd. Yet it was the goal scorers who were the lords of the field and of their city.

It needed a rare and thrilling ability to beat the system and Charles had all the talents to score goals or stop them. It was little wonder that he reached the height of his fame and fortune in Turin, or that he identified himself closely with the town of his adoption to become part-owner of one of its best-known restaurants. The only surprise was his decision to return to Leeds, and an unhappy decision it was. His wife, Peggy, was a Leeds girl and the education of his children was the dominant motive. But for his career it was a sad blow. So keen were Juventus to keep him that they offered £18,000 for a single season. Quietly determined as always, Charles was not deflected from his purpose. Yet the sweet scent of success suddenly turned sour. The triumphal return degenerated into bitterness and criticism.

What went wrong? In part it was the difficulty of readjustment to English method with its different demands and different training. Charles might have been warned by his more recent experiences with Wales. The Italian Football League were loathe to release him and, without previous practice, his team mates now found his style hard to fathom or follow. Even in Sweden, for the World Cup Finals, it needed a couple of matches before he could settle back to their pattern of play. So it was with Leeds. To heighten the contrast he had been following Italian training methods. These put the emphasis on ball control and on suppleness of body; on quick starting, rather than staying power. English tactics and English pitches dictated a different approach with the concentration still on stamina. By these more exacting standards Charles was not fit enough and the quicker pace of the game prevented any smooth adjustment. He missed the close support and close understanding of the Italian players and his team-mates found it hard to respond to his methods. No doubt, he could have settled to his stride in time. But he was given no time, no respite.

Once again he was the victim of his own greatness. The advance publicity demanded quick results and sensational results. The failure to achieve them reaped a storm of criticism and misunderstanding. From the easy dominance of Italy to the harsh rejection at home was a shattering experience even for so phlegmatic a man as Charles. Soon he was yearning for Italy's warm climate and warm approbation. It needed only an offer from Roma to send him back. Once more Leeds were in pocket on the deal, but for Charles it marked the beginning of the decline that lead finally to the Southern League. He took the decision without regret 'I hope now everyone is satisfied. I will be because I have learned my lesson. Italy is the place for me. Italian football is the football for me. That is why I am going back.' Going back indeed he was for never again would he attain the same pinnacle of performance and reputation.

For Roma he could work no miracles and a year later they sold him to Cardiff City for £40,000 less than they had paid for the great man. In the next three seasons Cardiff had valuable service from him but he was no longer the irresistible goal scorer of old and found it increasingly difficult to hold his place in the side. So he moved on to Hereford and back to centre-half where the pace is less testing. In top class soccer he had scored 270 goals as well as proving himself a great centre-half. He was an outstanding product of British football, but it was Italy that made him internationally famous, a player of World class and World reputation.

Like any migrant, he achieved success by accepting with enthusiasm the manners and methods of the country of his adoption. Because he was ready to learn and adapt, he was able to teach and to add. He gave a new dimension to Italian soccer on the field. Off it he was able to enjoy or tolerate the personal adulation, or the scurrilous personal attack that is the lot of most celebrities. Unlike Jimmy Greaves, he accepted the traditions he found, rather than fight them. He was in love with their game as well as with their money. Most cricket fans enjoy the pleasurable pastime of selecting the best World cricket XI. It is a happy hobby good for hours of friendly discussion and an eternity of disagreement but, so far, soccer supporters seem to have evaded its spell. For any who do set about choosing the best ever British XI, John Charles must be an automatic selection, the argument centering on where, rather than whether, he should play. My own preference is for his power as a striker, rather than a stopper. It is a more exacting and exciting task, a more difficult role to fill with his distinction.

With Mel Charles he might also lay claim to the most effective brotherly combination in International football. That is a more difficult choice, but my own vote would go to Jack and Bobby Charlton, both of whom measure up to John Charles' giant stature, both of whom have an equal reputation in World football.

As a player to watch or analyse and as a personality, there seemed an endearing simplicity about John Charles. He was always direct and dependable, lacking only a hard edge to his nature and his prowess. His natural skills were enhanced by his physical attributes. Yet his career and his play have been at times surprisingly complex and inconsistent. He never dominated Welsh football as he dominated the Italian scene. He did not always produce his best in the vital games, or maintain a uniformly high level of performance. Perhaps versatility has its limits. The constant change of position, of place and of method extended his range, but complicated his problems. Inevitably it led to a lack of orientation, a lack of simplicity. It is this that John Charles has rediscovered at the close of his career and that leaves him serenely content with Hereford. One thing has never changed. Throughout his playing days he has sustained his sportsmanship, pure and unfaltering in the face of challenge. John Charles was a man of the fifties. That was the decade in which he bestrode the soccer world. It is too late now for him to recover a place at the top and we can look back to give verdict on the days of his dominance. Few have made so wide an impact on soccer. By his personal achievements he sustained British prestige when we were on the verge of forfeiting the respect of other nations. By his example he showed how to adapt and use the new ideas of Europe. By his own unique talent he disproved the theory that in soccer an outsize physique is a hindrance rather than a help.

As a final epitaph on his greatness it is enough to reiterate that he was once the individual target of the World Cup tacticians. There is no greater or more dangerous compliment than that.

SEVEN

Duncan Edwards
by Arthur Walmsley

ON A SUNNY DAY in the small Worcestershire town of Dudley, the red of Manchester United and the white of England beam from a stained-glass window in the church of St. Francis. The sharp rays soften to lend their own enrichment to the dappled, rainbow irradiation of the little cosmos within St. Francis's. It is a church window unique in Britain – probably in the world – for it glorifies a footballer among the saints.

From the top two of the window's four sections, St. George and St. Francis gaze down benignly on twin figures of Duncan Edwards depicted in soccer strip – one figure in the red of Manchester United, the other in the colours of his country. To the bigot it may seem an appalling alliance – incongruous at best, irreverent at worst – the canonised paired in their hushed and hallowed place with a professional practitioner of that game, according to legend, devised for gentlemen but played by ruffians.

The Bishop of Worcester, the Right Reverend Mervyn Charles-Edwards, brought no such bigotry to his dedication of the memorial window to Duncan Edwards on August 27th 1961. The Bishop said: 'Duncan and players like him have given people all over the world a fine example of the British way of life. I am sure that instead of constant meetings between the politicians which seem to increase tension, we could solve the Berlin situation much more easily by sending over football teams for a tournament.'

If events on the football fields of Europe since then have tended to devalue the Bishop's high assessment of football as an international peacemaker, they have not diminished the stature of Duncan Edwards, nor debased the Bishop's tribute.

Duncan's tragic death fourteen days after suffering multiple injuries in the Munich air crash on February 6th 1958, when Manchester United's charter plane failed to clear the runway on take-off, put him beyond the sordid wranglings of latter day football. And, if the Bishop had the shameful symbolism of the Berlin Wall more in mind than football in his reference to the former German capital, for me it will always be Duncan Edwards and his finest hour and not the inhumanities of opposing ideologies that will spring first to mind on the mention of 'Berlin.'

Since Duncan's death, the elation of that recollection has been tinged with poignancy, yet I recount the story in fullest detail here because I believe it crystallises the greatness of Duncan Edwards and prepares the way for a deeper appreciation of the biography that follows.

My Berlin story starts in Stockholm in mid-May, 1956. I was a member of the usual camp-following Press party with the England soccer team beginning a close-season tour which, from Sweden, was to take us to Finland and then to Berlin for the ultimate test against the, then, World Champions, West Germany. The party had left England under a storm of criticism. Team manager Walter Winterbottom had come under withering fire from sportswriters, including me, for scorning the genius of Stanley Matthews and Tom Finney in favour of the more functional football of wingers Colin Grainger and Gordon Astall.

It seemed unthinkable that we should be showing the flag abroad without the two brightest jewels in our soccer crown. There were others in the England party, too, whose inclusion seem to owe more to mere competence and a willingness to conform to Winterbottom's tactical instruction rather than to outstanding ability.

Winterbottom, in pursuit of his beloved soccer theory, was flirting dangerously with the country's sporting prestige – or so it seemed at the time. Looking back, and with England's 1966 World Cup triumph especially in mind, it is now easier to be sympathetic to Winterbottom's plan. In essence it was founded on the same reasoning as Sir Alfred Ramsey's – the preference for a balanced, blended team playing to a pre-conceived tactical plan rather than reliance on the extempore play and virtuosity of two or three star players with the rest fitting in as best they can. The vital difference between the application of that reasoning was that Sir Alfred had four years to perfect his plan – Winterbottom did not have as many weeks.

The opening match of the tour, against Sweden, confirmed our worst fears that Winterbottom had blundered. There was little of team blend or tactical competence to compensate for the lack of virtuosity as we struggled to a 1–1 draw against a team of enthusiastic, but mediocre, Swedish part-timers.

It was even worse in Helsinki. England won 5–1 – but against a Finnish eleven of a quality barely up to our own semi-professional league standards there was more disgrace in conceding a goal than honour in scoring five.

So we flew to Germany, to face the World Champions, resigned to the worst. But we were only thinking of the 'worst' in a football

DUNCAN EDWARDS 'His appetite for football was insatiable. Though sophisticated beyond his years in style, his approach to football never lost the eagerness of youth'

DANNY BLANCHFLOWER 'As a footballer, one could only admire
him; it seems to me that he was indisputably a great player, with
a vision of the game which was at once sophisticated yet simple; the
qualities of the very best football'

context. What those of us who had not been in Germany since the end of the war in 1945 did not know was that the test in Berlin had assumed a significance in the German mind far beyond the game of soccer.

The warning signs were clear on our arrival in Hanover where we were to stay for several days before moving to Berlin. We were quickly made to realise that the occupation of their country was deeply resented by the Germans. We met with dumb insolence in our own hotel and with open hostility in public places outside it. Indeed, on our third day in Hanover, one normally mild-mannered English sportswriter, standing barely 5 feet 6 inches with his heavy boots on, was so provoked in a café as to assault a giant German and actually get the better of him after first squaring up to his tormentor in classical old-time prize-fighter's pose and warning him 'he must not say things like that about the English.'

But the Hanover incidents paled as minor irritations when we arrived at the Olympic Stadium, Berlin for the first trial of soccer strength between West Germany and England on German soil since the war.

The Germans, perhaps understandably, were grasping at straws to retrieve their almost mortally-wounded national pride following the humiliation of defeat in the war and the subsequent carving up and occupation of their country. Their unexpected World Cup victory in 1954 had pointed soccer as the way the Germans could most swiftly restore some vestige of national self-respect. And now had come the chance to square accounts with the old enemy.

Before the Berlin match I had always deplored the nationalism which was becoming a rapidly increasing evil in sport. Imbued with the Corinthian spirit of putting the game beyond the prize, I had taken up a position outside nationalism, even when England was concerned, and had persistently preached the policy that it was better to lose well than win badly.

My starry-eyed idealism took a sickening jolt as I took my seat in the Olympic Stadium press box. Of the 90,000 capacity crowd, some 6,000 British occupation troops bravely waved their patriotic banners in pathetically tiny 'islands' surrounded by a heaving sea of Germans whose regimented baying and chanting made a shattering assault on the ears.

The near-hysteria of the Germans was almost tangible and unnervingly unhealthy. Here were all the frightening, ugly undertones

I

of those pre-war Nuremberg rallies; a people reduced to robots in the insane pursuit of superiority. Inevitably we caught the infection of nationalism. As our apprehension grew, we exaggerated the inadequacies of our team and the yearning for the absent Matthews and Finney, who might have brought this arrogant crowd to its knees, became unbearable.

The game began to an accompaniment of an even more deafening explosion of expectation from the crowd. The German team, captained and generalled by that master schemer Fritz Walter, rose to their compatriots and soon had us cursing Winterbottom's folly.

The brilliant Fritz Walter ripped our team apart with passes of metrical perfection and, as our disorganised defence desperately packed our penalty area, I knew a humiliation and depression of spirit I could hitherto never have believed could be associated with sport. The torment lasted some twenty minutes with the crowd screaming itself hoarse in frenzied impatience for that first goal which would surely be the forerunner of a floodtide.

Then it happened – the most spellbinding, dramatic experience of my sporting career. With pressure on the England goal fleetingly eased, the Goliath-like figure of young Duncan Edwards moved on to the ball some fifteen yards inside his own half. Three German players were dispositioned at regular intervals in the long, direct line between Edwards and the German penalty area. Initially, it seemed a situation of no especial significance.

Then Edwards began to move. The first German challenge was brushed contemptuously aside by the sheer power of Edwards's mounting surge. The second German tackled thin air as the youngster body-swerved past him. The third, attempting a head-on confrontation, merely bounced off the boy now in full cry for goal. Yet Edwards, with uncanny instinct, did not tempt the fates too far. Before over-running into the populated German penalty area he unleashed a shot of staggering ferocity from full twenty-five yards and the ball was straining the back of the net almost before the goalkeeper could move.

Emotion was naked. Tears sprang spontaneously to my eyes. In wild, unreasoning joy I wanted to break out of the press box and scream at every shocked and silent German 'Have you got a boy of nineteen who could do that?'

It was a magnificent assertion of authority against all the odds that I never expect to see again in sport from a man – much less a boy. Of course the occasion, with its lunatic nationalism, exalted a truly great goal to the realms of immortality. But of more immediate concern here is that it was a goal only Duncan Edwards could have scored.

It was a goal of a man, not a boy, yet it had its roots in the sublime self-confidence of youth. It was the goal of a Titan; the goal of an unconquerable heart. Only Duncan Edwards, of all the players I have seen, had all those qualities at nineteen.

The goal was also a catalyst precipitating a memorable England victory. England's men, inspired by the boy among them raised their game to heights beyond their normal powers and won 3–1.

I did not know it then, but that Berlin visit was to have a second, deeper, significance for me. As we flew out from Templehoff airport the day after our victory, Duncan Edwards remained behind. He was still doing National Service and was due to play in Germany with the British Army team. He came to see us off and, as we taxied to the runway, I peered through the porthole to take a last look at the unassuming youngster dressed unspectacularly in mufti – dark slacks, open-necked shirt and drab cardigan. The lone, wistful-looking figure leaning against a hangar door and waving us off looked the typical 'boy-next-door' – a sharp contrast to the heroic young god of soccer who had stunned Berlin to silence the night before.

As I watched him, I confess, there was envy in my heart. At nineteen he was already astride his chosen world. Already he was the Crown Prince of English football – Stanley Matthews had not yet abdicated as King – and in the years to come it seemed that in the gladsome pursuit of the game he so passionately loved, he would surely rule the world. My own youth was well behind me – but I wished with all my heart that I were Duncan Edwards. When Duncan died only two years later I remembered my envy and shivered a little with shame. Ever since it has helped me curb, if not entirely conquer, covetousness.

I have taken so much space to tell my Berlin story in order to illustrate the greatness of Edwards in mind as well as body. For his was a genius which flourished no matter how big or small the occasion.

His appetite for football was insatiable. Though sophisticated beyond his years in style, his approach to football never lost the eagerness of youth. Perhaps that is why his performance was as consistently outstanding as the frailty of humanity allows.

Psychologists and sociologists could have seen in Duncan Edwards more vividly than in any other of his generation at the time, the early portents of that surging, irrepressible determination for self-expression and self-reliance of the post-war teenager which – for better or worse – has set the modern youth apart from the generations that have gone before.

Duncan Edwards was born in Dudley on October 1st, 1936 and long before he left school had upset all the notions of natural progression in football. When he left primary school at eleven to join Wolverhampton Street Secondary Modern, his reputation as a footballer preceded him. A youngster reported to the sportsmaster that 'a smashing centre-half' was joining the school. The sportsmaster quickly saw – was even more quickly conquered – and, while only eleven, Edwards was picked for the Dudley Town Boys Team, four years before the usual age. They made a concession to his tender years – they played him at outside-left 'to keep him out of trouble.'

It was at this time that he came under the influence of his first, and perhaps most important mentor, Mr Eric Booth, secretary of the Dudley Schools F.A., to whom Duncan paid generous tribute in later years. Mr Booth's instruction to the schoolboy Edwards was simple and fundamental, but I believe it laid the solid foundation of Edwards's future greatness. He told the boy two things.

First – 'never hold the ball when you can part, then run into an open space for the return.' Unoriginal, maybe, but instruction of the first magnitude to a boy so abundantly gifted and whose game, both then and later, could have been rendered so much less effective had he succumbed to the natural temptations of the prodigy to 'go it alone.' But Edwards never forgot that early discipline and to the end was an exemplary team man.

Second – Mr Booth brainwashed Duncan into the necessity for being completely two-footed. Edwards took his instruction so much to heart in his formative years that in practice games in the local park at night he used only his 'swinger', his left foot, to kick with until he had developed a left as good as his right.

What rich rewards accrued from that particular piece of boyhood dedication! The power and accuracy of Duncan's crossfield pass has, in my experience, never been approached.

From his normal position at left half-back, the crossfield pass was hit with the left foot without any warning shift of balance yet with such velocity and accuracy that the first the opposition knew that play had been switched from one side of the pitch to the more vulnerable opposite was Edwards's right winger moving to take the ball in his stride. Of all Duncan's stratagems this was the most perfectly executed and the most telling.

Mr Booth was not long in recommending his young protégé for selection for the England schoolboy team and, with the same seeming inevitability that every other representative honour in the game came his way, Duncan was shortly making his first acquaintance with Wembley as a schoolboy international. In time he captained the team and in all played nine times over two seasons – a record likely to stand for all time.

But even as Edwards's schoolboy career was beginning to take shape, his professional one was already being plotted. The tale is worth telling, if only to illustrate the thoroughness and far-sighted team-building which has made Manchester United, under Sir Matt Busby's managership, the greatest English club in post-war football.

When Edwards was only twelve he was watched by Manchester United's Midlands representative, Reg Priest, who immediately reported back in glowing terms that he had seen a certain star of the future. At that time professional clubs were not allowed to approach schoolboys nor sign a boy until he was sixteen. So during the next four years Reg Priest patiently and diligently plotted Duncan's progress and reported regularly to the club. In all, Priest watched Edwards twenty times.

Then, late on the night of September 30th, 1952, Matt Busby left Manchester by car for Dudley. He arrived soon after midnight at the Edwards' home – just a few minutes after the sleeping youngster had become sixteen. After talks with Duncan's father, the boy was roused from his sleep at 2 a.m. and told to come downstairs as he had a visitor. The puzzled, sleepy-eyed youngster shot awake when he saw the visitor was Matt Busby. The dazzling prospect of joining England's most glamorous club almost overwhelmed the lad, and he signed the contract form without hesitation.

Though Reg Priest had painted Duncan's 'pedigree' in glowing colours and his appearances as a schoolboy international had had all the professional clubs in the country drooling over him, there was no special treatment for the young Edwards at Old Trafford. It was not Busby's way to pamper one boy above another. Edwards moved into digs in Manchester with eight other young United hopefuls. For a time he worked during the day learning joinery and trained two hours each Tuesday and Thursday night. As a member of the ground staff he was paid a modest fifty-shillings a week and did his share of boot-cleaning for the senior professionals.

Only nine months after leaving school, however, and six months after joining Manchester United, he made his First Division debut. It was no planned affair. There was no big public relations promotion preceding the launching of the schoolboy wonder in the big-time of professional football.

On Saturday morning, April 4th, 1953, Edwards turned up at Old Trafford as usual, but this time to learn that Henry Cockburn, United's England international left half-back was unable to play in the League home game with Cardiff City because of injury.

'Go back home and get your boots, son,' said Matt Busby, 'you're playing in the first team.' In terms of the result it was not a happy debut day. Manchester United were beaten 4–1. Yet even in decisive defeat Edwards showed he was worthy to take his place alongside such established masters as Johnny Carey, Jack Rowley and Stan Pearson.

Edwards was in the United team to stay. At seventeen he signed full professional forms for the club and almost immediately was picked for the England Under-23 team. He played six times for the Under-23 team – that number only being limited because he 'grew' out of it long before others, years older, had got in.

The Under-23 team was essentially a testing and proving ground for future full international players, and Edwards had already arrived at that ultimate honour by the time he was eighteen years six months. At that age he was picked for the full England team to play against Scotland at Wembley – in 1954 – and is the youngest player ever to be 'capped' by England.

His England debut had a happier conclusion than the one for his club. England, with Stanley Matthews destroying Scotland almost single-handed on his favourite playground, won 7–2.

Edwards was subsequently never dropped by England. The only matches he missed between his first selection and his death were due to injury. In all he won eighteen full 'caps'. He also made four England 'B' team appearances – an open age team regarded as an intermediary step between the Under-23 and full England teams and now defunct.

Edwards won League championship medals with his club in 1956 and 1957, but 1957 also proved the year of the one great disappointment of his career. Manchester United had reached the F.A. Cup Final, and with the League Championship cup already decorating the boardroom, they seemed the nearest thing to achieve the modern miracle of Cup and League double.

It was all Wembley to a public park pitch that the mighty United stars would sweep an indifferent Aston Villa aside in the Cup Final. Fortune, however, is never more fickle than in its dealings with 'certainties' in soccer. The balance of power in the final was dramatically upset shortly after the start when the Villa left winger, Peter McParland, collided with United goalkeeper Ray Wood. As a result, Wood fractured a cheek bone and was led off the field concussed. Centre-half Jackie Blanchflower, brother of Danny of Tottenham Hotspur fame, took over in goal and the inevitable Edwards switched to centre-half.

Even now, it seemed, Manchester United had an abundance of talent to overcome this serious handicap. They held out until half-time, but two shock goals by that ace 'poacher', McParland, knocked the psychological stuffing out of the Champions.

Wood made a brave but brief token appearance on the wing where he wandered dazedly to little purpose. Edwards, pulling on every ounce of his giant strength and stamina, strove valiantly to make up the missing link and when Tommy Taylor headed a late goal for United from a corner it was centre-half Edwards who took the corner. But the presentiment of defeat had United in its grip and Villa ran out worthy 2–1 winners.

How ironical that the following year at Wembley, Stan Crowther, who had played a prominent part in Villa's triumph over United, should find himself filling Duncan Edwards's left-half position in the Old Trafford line-up. United, only three months after Munich, had astonishingly reached the Cup Final again – aided by the emergency signings of former England international Ernie Taylor, from Blackpool, and Crowther.

This time, however, Crowther was to know the heartbreak of defeat as United, emotionally spent, went under 2–0 to a Bolton Wanderers side inspired by that old England campaigner Nat Lofthouse. An F.A. Cupwinners' medal, therefore, was the only major honour to elude the incredible Edwards in a four-and-a-half-year professional career during which he blazed across the soccer heavens with the brilliance and brevity of a comet.

What were the ingredients of his greatness? It would be easy to fall into the trap of ascribing his dominance to sheer physical strength. Doubtless his exceptional physique – 5ft 10½in and 12½ stone – as a sixteen-year-old gave him distinct advantage over those of similar age. He had legs like young oaks and a torso like a miniature tank.

It was an advantage he was never reluctant to exploit. Edwards was no gentle giant. He tackled for keeps, and meeting him in a head-on clash must have been a bone-shattering experience. If the dispositions were not suited for sheer ball play or constructive distribution, Edwards, in a tight corner, would bulldoze through opponents by sheer brute force.

Sheer strength alone, however, would not have been enough to elevate him to the highest soccer company in the land as a boy playing with men. Much more important than the physical in his make-up was the mental. Edwards had a soccer brain years in advance of his age and brought the almost arrogant poise and temperament of a veteran to his game. He was a magnificent header of a ball and could dribble with an easy artistry which belied the bulk of his considerable frame.

Above all he had presence; his play bore the stamp of awesome authority. Almost everything he did, whether performing a rescue act in defence; inspiring attack; or surging through his own forwards to save a lost cause with a thunderbolt drive; had purpose. He scorned over-elaboration. It was the sheer economy of his work and the austere control of his multi-various talents that made him such a priceless asset to club and country.

His versatility – in his own time – was matched only by the great John Charles, although Johnny Carey, who retired soon after Edwards made his League debut for Manchester United, left a record of versatility which will surely never be equalled at Old Trafford or any other club. In 346 matches for Manchester United, though it was at right full-back that Carey established himself as a defender of peerless artistry, he played in all but two positions – outside-right and outside-left. To greater or lesser degree he filled each of the nine positions with distinction.

To complete the record I should add that he did play outside-right in the reserve team. Edwards was never called on to emulate that record but he was always Matt Busby's ace-in-the-hole in emergency or in some specific tactical plan. He could switch with equal facility and effect from his normal position of left half-back to centre-half, full-back or inside-forward and was not infrequently required to do so.

Edwards's early death has left the eternal question: How great would he have been had he lived? Frankly, my own mind boggles at the prospect of a steadily improving Duncan Edwards as experience brought even greater sophistication of mind and ability to the player already head and shoulders above the host of his contemporaries. The logical conclusion is that he would have so grown in stature as to dwarf those around him and leave us unfairly sceptical of their ability.

Yet, as not infrequently happens in sport, the player who was such a powerfully commanding figure on the field was a quiet, self-effacing character off it. He had little relish for the ballyhoo and personal publicity that went with being a national soccer figure and was never happier, off field, than when he could get away for a quiet day's fishing. He often asked to be excused after-match banquets so that he could escape to the anonymity of his lodgings, but never showed annoyance on the occasions when permission was refused because it was felt he should attend.

In the dressing-room he never attempted a life-and-soul-of-the-party role but was enough of a professional to let down his natural reserve and make his own contribution to team spirit with a dry wit.

When the team sheet went up each Friday he never expressed surprise or discontent whatever position he was shown to be filling. It was enough for Edwards that he was in the team. And if that seems a minor virtue, take this nine-day period in February, 1955, which would surely have strained the forbearance of almost any other player beyond the limit.

In the local 'derby' game against Manchester City Edwards started at left half-back. When Allenby Chilton was sent off Edwards moved to centre-half. A few days later he was due to play centre-forward in the Manchester United youth team – Busby's ace-in-the-hole in a bid to retain the F.A. Youth Cup which the club had won in the previous two years since the inception of the competition. But results had been going against the first team and so Edwards was pulled out of the youth side and picked inside-left for the seniors. He was injured in the first half of that game and played the whole of the second half at outside-right!

When Edwards was called up for National Service in August, 1955, it seemed his professional career would be badly disrupted, but after initial training in the Royal Army Ordnance Corps at Portsmouth, he was posted to a munitions depot at Shrewsbury, only a two-hour run from Manchester, where the commanding officer, Colonel 'Sam' Orton, a soccer enthusiast, took a most benevolent view of Edwards being released for Manchester United games.

Not surprisingly, there was more soccer than soldiering in Duncan's National Service. He was in demand for unit, regional and full Army games as well as for club and country fixtures. It seems almost a contradiction in terms to tie the name of Duncan Edwards to a surfeit of soccer – yet he must have come perilously close to it during the 1956-57 season. By the end of the season he had played 94 club and representative games in addition to the small stuff with his unit. Nearing physical and mental exhaustion, he still had a close season tour of the Iron Curtain countries to come with the England Under-23 team.

There was the additional strain of flying, of which he was never fond, and on the flight to the last match of the tour against the Czech Under-23 team in Bratislava he looked drawn and weary. Edwards could easily have pleaded fatigue and been excused playing, but that would have been against his very nature. He played and scored both England's goals with scorching drives in a 2–0 win.

So we come to the last, sad chapter in the Duncan Edwards story. There would be no excuse for recounting the last few harrowing days of his life if it did not dignify his memory or reveal by fact, rather than opinion, the high regard and deep admiration he had excited not only in his own country but throughout Europe and beyond during his tragically short career.

When Manchester United's plane crashed at Munich on February 6th, 1958, killing eight of his team-mates, three club officials and nine sportswriters, Duncan Edwards was cruelly injured. He had a compound fracture of the right thigh, broken ribs, a collapsed lung, a broken pelvis and was in a state of severe shock. A lesser man would never have been carried from the plane alive.

Yet for those of us who waited, there seemed hope that the injuries would not prove fatal. We knew the young giant's strength and fighting heart, and for five days there were no alarming reports from the Munich hospital where a brilliant team under Professor Maurer were performing miracles of life-saving and forging a permanent link of friendship between the cities of Munich and Manchester.

It was on February 11th that we first learned Edwards might not live. His kidneys had also been badly injured in the crash and were now beginning to fail. An artificial kidney machine was rushed 210 miles to Munich by road from Freiburg and following its application Edwards was reported as 'amazingly better though still gravely ill.'

On February 13th he was well enough to talk to his parents and the news inspired new hope that all would yet be well. Meanwhile, as Duncan's kidney condition became widely known, moving offers of sacrifice reached the Munich hospital. One woman in Johannesburg, who had been born with two pairs of kidneys, offered her spare set to Edwards. Four other offers of a kidney came from two Germans, a Frenchman and a Belgian. All the offers had to be refused because of the virtual certainty that a graft would not be successful.

On February 17th, the kidney machine was needed again, but its effectiveness decreased. As the machine washed the non-protein nitrogen content from Duncan's blood it also reduced the ability of the blood to clot. He had severe haemorrhages and despite five blood transfusions gradually sank into a coma and died peacefully on February 21st.

At last the valiant heart that had fought the impossible fight was still. Dr Graham Taylor, British European Airways medical officer said: 'Only his tremendous physical strength and powerful fighting spirit kept him going. He was an amazing man. No ordinary person would have survived so long.'

Duncan Edwards was buried on February 26th. Thousands lined the funeral route and police had to divert traffic in Dudley. The church of St. Francis could hold only a few of those who wished to pay their last tribute to this splendid son of England and the service was relayed to the parish hall. Among the pall bearers were Duncan's former England team colleagues Billy Wright, Ray Barlow, Don Howe and Ron Clayton.

A special headstone made from black Swedish granite and fashioned by Aberdeen craftsmen adorns the grave. An action picture from a Press photograph showing Duncan poised for one of his long throw-ins is worked on the black stone. The headstone was unveiled by Matt Busby, himself a survivor of severe injuries at Munich, in October, 1958, and has since become a sporting shrine. Regularly those who remember or have read of him come from all parts of the country to pay silent tribute to the footballer who personified all that was best in his country.

This appreciation of Duncan Edwards would be incomplete, however, without an epilogue from the two men who, outside his family, mourn him most. They are Matt Busby and his assistant manager Jimmy Murphy. Almost a decade after Duncan's death I asked them how they now saw the player who had seemed unique in his time. Had distance lent even further enchantment or had the startling emergence of youth in first class football in the years since Duncan's death done something to diminish the image?

An assumed professional toughness and a natural Celtic high emotion are constantly at war in Jimmy Murphy. The mere mention of Duncan Edward's name was enough to bring tears to his eyes. There was a pause for self-control, then Murphy breathed emotionally: 'The greatest thing on two legs – then, now and always. He was as fine an example off the field as he was on. Never gave us a moment's trouble. I've seen great half-backs in my time – Copping, MacKay, Paul, and many more – but never one to touch Duncan Edwards. And he'd only just begun . . .' Murphy had to leave it there.

Matt Busby, too, had to stifle emotion when I asked him how he rated Edwards now. There was a sort of reverence in his voice as he said: 'What can I say? When he joined us he was only sixteen yet there was nothing we had to teach him. Time after time we watched him in match and practice, searching for some fault we might help him to correct. But we could find none. He was complete.'

In the thoroughbred Soccer 'stable' of Manchester United they could teach the young 'colt' Edwards nothing. Even in this selective pantheon of Soccer gods surely they do not come any greater than that.

EIGHT

Danny Blanchflower
by Brian Glanville

I F ONE were to seek for the watershed between the old school of professional footballer and the new, one might do worse than look at Danny Blanchflower. Not that he was, in any strict sense, representative of either; merely that, as a great player of uncommon intelligence and versatility, he suffered under the regimen which ended with the New Deal of 1961, while suggesting to those who came after it what they might become. By 1961, the erosion of social difference which followed our bloodless social revolution had already given pro footballers a much less working class orientation than they'd had before the war. They no longer dressed in baggy suits, mufflers and cloth caps, no longer felt content with an Andy Capp life a few rungs higher than Andy Capp himself, their fan, might have. But Blanchflower, fluent to a fault, articulate to a paradox, fraternising with literary editors and philosophers, writing for the intellectual weeklies and the posh Sundays, pointed the way to wider horizons still. Thus, though he played little or no active part in the crusade to abolish the iniquitous maximum wage, in 1960 and 1961, he had already given the pro footballer a new concept of himself; or what he might, in some remote future, become.

It is hard for me to write about Blanchflower, because I have known him for many years, and moderately closely. I say moderately closely, because Blanchflower is not an easy man to know well. The charm, the eloquence, mask rather than illuminate; there is a core of something secret, held back, concealed. Thus, one can say of him that he is intelligent, humorous, ambitious, competitive, even egocentric, but the inwardness of the man is elusive.

As a footballer, one could only admire him; it seems to me that he was indisputably a great player, with a vision of the game which was at once sophisticated yet simple; the qualities of the very best football. It was these characteristics which enabled him to be so fine a captain, at a time when football captaincy had grown to be little more than a question of tossing for ends before the kick-off. The freshness and originality of his approach to the game, combined with his remarkable poise, enabled him to give a team inspiration, confidence, and a sense of tactical purpose. He did it superbly with Tottenham Hotspur – and for a time, significantly, had the captaincy taken away from him. He did it just as well with

143

a Northern Ireland team which, against all expectation, knocked Italy out of the eliminators for the 1958 World Cup, and reached the quarter-finals.

It has been said, possibly with truth, that the dominant force in his life has been his mother; once the pretty centre-forward of a women's football team, and Blanchflower's first coach. He was born and brought up in that hard, vigorous, bigoted city, Belfast, 'where they beat the big drum,' as he once said; but there is nothing bigoted about him. He seems to have inherited the city's vigorous, robust humour, with none of its black undertones. He began there with Glentoran, joined Barnsley, in Yorkshire, as little more than a boy, from there went to Aston Villa and finally, in 1954, joined Spurs, thus coming to London, where he must always have felt he belonged, where there was an opportunity to grow, to prosper and to spread himself.

If one were to describe him, as a player, in one word, I suppose that word would be 'scientific.' Certainly he owed nothing to force. Wiry and fit, he carried little weight, and though he did not flinch from tackles, it was his positional play, his highly developed sense of anticipation, which made him remarkable. Nor was he ever very quick – except in thought. And if there were some who criticised his defensive qualities, it might be answered that he was a little unfortunate to come slightly before what would have been 'his' time; that of 4–2–4, and the specialised mid-field man. I remember, just after he had come back from the World Cup of 1958, his speaking enthusiastically to me in that great, grey clearing house of gossip and opinion, the Tottenham car park, of 4–2–4. What a good and simple idea it was, he said, simply to string a line of four defenders right across the pitch.

He was even, in season 1958-59, dropped from the Tottenham Hotspur team, and replaced by some young half-back whose name one can barely remember, on the grounds that he was not defensive enough. When, in March, 1959, he came back, it was to inspire the team to a marvellous six goal victory against Leicester City. You will deduce, from this, that he had to suffer a lot of pain for his uniqueness, his vigorous non-conformity. At Barnsley, at Aston Villa, then at Tottenham, he was never free from the reminder that he was, in the last analysis, a professional footballer, a paid servant.

It was at Barnsley, for example, that someone yelled at him for daring to be so unorthodox as to train with the ball. It would be many years before the Hungarians came to Wembley, thrashed England 6–3, and paved the way for a general acknowledgement that it really might be better to prepare for a ball game with a ball. Even as a youngster newly arrived in England, Blanchflower was shrewd enough to doubt the value of continued lapping, the mindless development of stamina. He has always believed – and it has come to be a heresy once more – that the great and dangerous forward may be dangerous precisely *because* he does so little; like a dormant volcano, always liable to erupt. This discussion, I recall, was provoked by a match against the Russian team, Tbilissi Dynamo. Their international outside-left, Meshki, had stood inactive on the wing for much of the time, but looked wonderfully effective when he did come to life. Today, when all is 'work rate,' a player like Meshki – or Greaves – might be considered a luxury. Blanchflower, always superbly economic himself, knew better.

One may see him today, perhaps, as a bruised idealist; not cynical, but hurt. Professional football is, to some degree, a paradigm of the larger world. Young players enter it full of hope and enthusiasm, only to encounter the proud stupidity of directors, the ineptitude of managers, the violence of opponents, the shallow ephemerality of the Press. Thus Blanchflower, particularly aware and alert, was hurt more than most professionals.

There was, for example, the shock, as a very young international, of having the team's coach invaded by jolly, ultra-convivial men who turned out to be . . . officials. Where was the sense of high minded purpose which he himself had brought to international football? And the awful anticlimax, the dazed disappointment, of the first international match in which he played.

It was in October, 1949, against Scotland, in Belfast; and Ireland let in eight goals. Those were bad days indeed for Ulster football. The team, subject in any case to the whims of the Football League clubs, who need not release their players if they did not choose, met at the eleventh hour, and took the field with little hope, little in the way of history.

The Irish team stayed in Bangor, and Blanchflower spent a wretched night, trying unavailingly to sleep. 'The nervous anticipation of the big event had something to do with that' he wrote. Then, in the small hours, when sleep seemed possible and imminent, a noisy band of Scottish fans arrived, and tore the peace of the night to tatters.

K

Blanchflower describes his recollections of that Saturday as 'mere shadows.' He was 'numb, dangling in a state of nervous suspension.' It is an interesting admission, given the absolute aplomb of his later career. Clearly he had none of the precocious *sang froid* of a Cliff Bastin or a Pelé who, as teenagers, could stroll untroubled through a Cup Final, or even a World Cup Final.

'The game that day,' wrote Blanchflower, in the *International Football Book,* 'swirled past me, over me, around me like a fog. I chased fleeting figures through it; but all in vain. I felt weak and exhausted as if I had no control over my movements; and everything I did seemed strangely irrelevant to the game.'

In parenthesis, the most intriguing thing about this passage is that it should be written by Blanchflower himself not, as in the case of almost every other footballer, by some assiduous 'ghost.' Blanchflower has a natural talent for writing as well as for football, but this is a subject to which I shall return later.

After the game, Blanchflower, 'slumped into the dressing-room, a pathetic figure sadly humiliated by bitter experience.' He was ashamed and disappointed at what he considered his total failure, and wondered if he would ever be chosen for his country again. Though there were excuses to lean on, he acknowledged that the main responsibility was his own. But he was well aware of the sad inertia which grips a losing team, of the whimsical methods of selection, of the lack of any leader to give the team direction and morale. At the same time, especially coming from the Second Division, he had been made to realise what a gap there was between club and international football, where there were so many good players about.

It was, by his own admission, Peter Doherty who recovered him for international football; Doherty who was one of the few figures in the game he has ever admired (another, I think, was Arthur Rowe, in his days as manager of Tottenham.)

Doherty had shared Blanchflower's resentment of the slapdash, defeatist way in which Irish teams were put in the field. Like Blanchflower, he was an individualist, often a stormy one, and a wonderfully talented player. 'Always remembering Doherty,' he once said, 'I aim at precision soccer. Constructiveness, no matter what the circumstances, ball control, precise and accurate distribution, back in defence to blot out the inside-forward when necessary. I am described as an attacking wing-half, and I suppose that is correct. Sometimes I even score goals.'

Doherty's appointment as team manager gave Ireland, and Blanchflower, new life. 'Here was someone', wrote Blanchflower, 'it seemed right should be in charge; a great player, an idol to some of us, a man we all respected. There was hope; something to believe in, something to fight for.' Doherty told them they had nothing to lose; 'the biggest step forward,' Blanchflower has said, 'was a psychological one.' This in turn led him to a developing interest in the psychological aspects of the game at large. Though the individual skills and abilities of the Irish team had improved, he was aware that what Doherty had done, above all, was to remove an enormous mental block. Once the Irish team had convinced itself that it was as good as anybody else, it proceeded to prove as much, on the field. The climax of Doherty's partnership with Blanchflower, if one may so describe what it virtually came to be, was reached in the 1958 World Cup.

Blanchflower, though his background was largely similar, had had a better formal education than Doherty. He was born in Bloomfield, a suburb of East Belfast, one street away from Billy Bingham, who would become his outside-right in that notable Irish team. Bingham and Danny's younger brother, Jackie, in fact, played together in the same boys' football team run by Mrs. Blanchflower, after at first playing football in the street; a game in which Danny sometimes joined.

Blanchflower went to the local college of technology, to be trained as an electrician. In 1944, however, volunteering for the Royal Air Force, he was sent to St. Andrew's University, for a short course in electrical engineering. It was a view into another, alien but beguiling world; the students, in their red gowns, represented a fortunate way of existence, a privilege of learning which had been denied to him. After this, he was subjected to another new experience, being sent to Canada for aircrew training. But the war was over, and he was still in Canada, before he could do any operational flying.

Returned to Belfast, Glentoran, with whom he had been an amateur, gave him £50 and £3 a match to sign professional, though until his demobilisation, he played as a 'guest' for Swindon Town. In 1948, Barnsley signed him, and three years later, they transferred him to Aston Villa, a great club fallen on barren times.

Blanchflower has related, often enough, the traumatising story of how he signed for Villa; travelling to Derby with Mr. Joe Richards, the coal-owner who was chairman of Barnsley and later President of the Football League, in his chauffeur-driven car – then, when they reached Derby, being sent with the chauffeur to eat in the kitchen, while business was done in the hotel dining-room. What was he, after all, but a professional footballer; and, as such, one consigned to the kitchen and the tradesmen's entrance? This, though Villa paid £15,000 for him.

Further disillusion lay in wait for him at Villa Park. Villa may have been a very great team indeed up to the Great War, a goodish one in the early twenties, but ever since their relegation in the thirties, they had been a stagnant, disappointing club. Playing for them, Blanchflower matured both physically and technically, but there was none of the stimulus a player of his capacities required, no manager there to inspire and lead him as Doherty had done, little chance, season by season, of anything better than staying in the middle reaches of the First Division.

In 1954, he agitated long enough for a transfer to get it. He wanted London; and London wanted him. Both the great North London clubs, Spurs and Arsenal, were eager to sign him. Tom Whittaker, the manager of Arsenal, came up to Villa Park, met Blanchflower, and told him that of course he would be coming to Highbury, that Arsenal could match or top any offer that was made. But in the event, they couldn't. The bidding rose to £30,000, a larger sum than had ever before been paid for a half-back, and Arsenal's board of directors refused to allow Whittaker to go so high. The same kind of penny-pinching would lose Arsenal Denis Law, when he was a £55,000 rather than £100,000 player. Blanchflower never forgot it. He was convinced from that moment that there was something rotten in the state of Arsenal – like Villa, a great club fallen on mediocre times – and his scepticism would flair into a silly row, twelve years later. After a somewhat intemperate article in the *Sunday Express* criticising Arsenal's treatment of an injured player, the club suspended him indefinitely from their Press Box.

Blanchflower has written amusingly of the cameo at Villa Park when he was due to be transferred; how the directors sat in the Board Room while he waited next door with a local journalist called Tommy Lyons, how it was Tommy Lyons, not Blanchflower, who was eventually and mistakenly called into the Board Room. Still, the transfer to Tottenham Hotspur went through, conducted by Arthur Rowe – who justified the price by saying, 'In nine matches out of ten, Blanchflower has the ball more than any other two players on the field – it's an expression of his tremendous ego, which is just what a great captain needs.'

From this you will divine not only that Rowe had a deep appreciation of Blanchflower's qualities, but that he was prepared to allow him to exercise them. In other words, he was a big enough man and manager himself to give Blanchflower free rein on the field; as a real captain. Yet Rowe, a sensitive, vigorous, idealistic, enormously stimulating man, had not much time to go at Tottenham. He had been bitterly wounded by the opposition and hostility of certain directors, manifested even during the most successful days of his push-and-run strategy.

The fact was, however, that Blanchflower was the last player to adapt himself to push and run. This game of wall passes, of immediate parting with the ball over short distances, was quite alien to his own, which was more deliberative. The beauty of push-and-run, in a way, was that it did not require any specific midfield general. Certainly Eddie Baily, the little English international inside-left, was a fine constructive player, but in fact, every player carried a field marshal's baton in his knapsack. Blanchflower liked to give the ball room and space; was always adept at chipping it, floating it, lobbing it. Endless, hurried movement was not for him; any more than it was for the brilliant little waif of an inside-forward, Tommy Harmer, a footballer's footballer who had been in and out of the Spurs first team for years, because he did not fit into the push-and-run formula.

Blanchflower and Harmer were to establish a marvellous, telepathic partnership. There could scarcely have been two more sharply contrasted figures. Though both had enormous technical talent, and what the Italians call 'a vision of the game,' Harmer did it all by instinct while Blanchflower, besides the natural good instincts of a fine player, had his ratiocinating intelligence, as well. He was from Belfast, Harmer was a Cockney of the Cockneys, uneasy anywhere too far from Hackney. Yet they combined marvellously, each perfectly understanding the needs and intentions of the other, and they set up some famous victories; not least one which brought ten goals against Everton.

There were moments, not least when Spurs were awarded a free kick, when they appeared to be arguing. 'They really *were* arguing,' said a London journalist who, like Harmer, came from Hackney. 'Tommy's quite serious about it; he says, "Got to keep Danny down, you know!"'

Later, the partnership with Harmer would give way to one with the marvellously elusive John White, 'The Ghost,' floating unobserved, by all but Blanchflower, into open spaces, unmarked positions, especially out on the left – where Blanchflower would reach him with impeccably accurate balls.

When Arthur Rowe, who had already been driven into one breakdown, had another and left the Spurs, he was succeeded by a very different manager; Jimmy Anderson. Anderson had, like Rowe – once a Tottenham captain – been with Spurs for many years, graduating from the position of third team trainer slowly and steadily up to manager. He was regarded essentially as an interim appointment; a figure without glamour or allure who, whatever hidden qualities he might have possessed, was unlikely to hit it off with a Blanchflower.

A crisis point was reached when Spurs lost to Manchester City, in the semi-final of the 1956 F.A. Cup, at Villa Park. Spurs, in the concluding stages, were behind, their attack making little impression on the City defence. In desperation, Blanchflower, in his capacity as captain, called the gigantic Maurice Norman, centre-half, up to inside-right. Norman was very tall, very heavy, rather clumsy, but undoubtedly a fearsome figure, particularly efficient in the air. The gamble might have worked, given a grain of luck; but it didn't. The other possibility, that of City exploiting a weakened defence, was the one which came about, and Tottenham lost, City went on to win the Cup.

Blanchflower was deprived of the captaincy, and for a long time, steadfastly refused to resume it. He was not going to be captain, he said, in name alone; either he exercised the rights of a captain, or someone else could have the job; or the sinecure. At the end of that season, he was even, briefly, dropped. The announcement was that he was unfit. Blanchflower said this was nonsense, he was perfectly fit. 'I turned up at White Hart Lane all ready to go. I thought the lads were kidding when they told me.'

In due course the dim interregnum of Jimmy Anderson came to

an end, but the manager who succeeded him was – if much more forceful – little nearer Blanchflower in temperament. Billy Nicholson had been a dour, conscientious right-half in the splendid push-and-run team, a Yorkshireman without frills or exaggerated ambitions, content to chase and tackle and cover till the cows came home. Some, cruelly, had said that he did Alf Ramsey's tackling for him. He was anything but a stupid man; his exceedingly shrewd tactical thinking had provided England with a plan to hold Brazil to a goalless draw in the Swedish World Cup of 1958; no other side had prevented Brazil scoring. But Nicholson, though subject to refreshing bursts of good humour, was in the main close, wary and cautious. Besides, a player of Blanchflower's stature and loquacity was not the easiest kind for a young manager to inherit. They had, inevitably their ups and downs, but in the end they worked together in sufficient harmony for Spurs brilliantly to achieve the League and Cup double which had eluded every other club in this century.

I don't think I myself saw Blanchflower play at all till the middle fifties – I had been living in Italy – and was not, initially, too impressed. He was, at the time, being used at inside-right, a position which manifestly did not suit him. He hadn't the acceleration, nor the ability to turn quickly, while his many qualities of foresight and construction largely went begging. He regained his rightful position, of course, and Spurs, buying Dave Mackay from Hearts, transferred their ultra-attacking left-half, Jim Iley.

Blanchflower and Mackay were to form a magnificent partnership. By utter contrast with Blanchflower, Mackay was all muscle and flamboyance, capable of what might loosely be termed 'tackles' (he was to sober down in time) which made one's hair stand on end. He clapped his hands, he stuck out his barrel chest: he took, *ad infinitum*, what Peter Cook once called 'his long, boring throwins,' he flung himself among flailing boots. He was essentially a hectic player, certainly not without skills, but with none of Blanchflower's cool, rational artistry. They complemented one another spendidly, though if I were asked which had the greater importance to the team I should reply, unhesitatingly, Blanchflower. This became very obvious when he retired, and Spurs all at once lost the direction and detachment which he had given them. Mackay, John White, Jimmy Greaves were all, in their way, remarkable footballers, but it was Blanchflower, finally, who gave the team its stamp and character.

I remember in particular a European Cupwinners' Cup game, at White Hart Lane, against Slovan, Bratislava. Spurs had lost the first leg, in Czechoslovakia, and they made a bad, nervous beginning. Maurice Norman, the centre-half, was clearly on edge, plunging and lunging at balls, committing himself and being drawn out of position. But there beside him was Blanchflower, like a groom calming a high-strung racehorse, slowing the game, covering mistakes, till at last Norman and the rest of the team settled down for an easy win.

Similarly, the triumphs of the 1957/58 Ireland side would have been unthinkable without Blanchflower; as they would have been equally impossible without Doherty. The team had in it a handful of very talented players, a few who were naturally gifted but unreflective, others who were frankly moderate. Among the most talented was Blanchflower's own brother, Jackie, at centre-half. A player of immense versatility, Jackie had begun with Manchester United as an inside-right, been turned into a right-half, and finally, with immense success, into a centre-half.

Danny admired him, as a footballer, a great deal, though they were temperamentally quite different; Jackie hadn't the same, consuming ambition as his older brother, and seemed prepared to make less stringent demands on life. In the 1957 Cup Final, when Manchester United's goalkeeper, Ray Wood, was injured, Jackie went in goal, and won Danny's admiration for the clever way he distributed the ball. Goalkeeper's distribution, indeed, has always been one of Danny's hobby horses. Given this, and his love of paradox, perhaps it was explicable that one day, in the Burnley team coach, he should reach a point where he seemed to be advocating distribution as the chief quality any goalkeeper needed, where others might feel that the first duty was to keep the ball out of the net!

One of the chief reasons Danny enjoyed playing for Ireland with Jackie was that his younger brother's great all-round skill and confidence allowed him to be left chiefly to his own devices. Danny himself could go upfield and occupy himself with the build-up in midfield. But in February, 1958, Jackie was involved in the appalling disaster of Munich Airport, when the Elizabethan air liner carrying Manchester United back from Belgrade crashed. Mercifully, Jackie himself escaped, but he was painfully injured, and never again graced a game for which he had been so well endowed.

This meant that Ireland had to find a new centre-half for the finals of the World Cup, in Sweden, and they manufactured one out of the tall, blond full-back, Willie Cunningham. Cunningham was a solid enough footballer, but he could aspire to none of Jackie Blanchflower's class, with the result that Danny had to play a much more cautious and defensive game. It is interesting – and rather sad – to speculate how much better Ireland might have done in Sweden, had Jackie Blanchflower played.

But the footballer who had the greatest affinity, both temperamentally and in his approach to the game, in that Irish team was Jimmy McIlroy. Dark haired, pink complexioned, modest and dry, McIlroy, at inside-forward, brought to football the same cool perfectionism, the emphasis on skill and science, as Blanchflower. They both thought about the game a great deal, they liked each other, perhaps a little warily – they were wonderfully humorous together – and they had the Irish team playing football their way; and Doherty's way. They delighted in working out new moves and strategies; such as the penalty-kick which involved both of them running into the area, the first pushing the ball forward for the other, following up, to shoot home. Blanchflower, as might be expected, was particularly good at taking penalties, success usually guaranteed by his cool composure.

On the right wing, the ebullient little Billy Bingham, later to become the Irish team manager, was a player of another mould, more of a force of nature. It was no use McIlroy and Blanchflower expecting Bingham to share their quizzical, rational approach to the game. If he had, no doubt they could have worked out some remarkable triangular schemes. But football is a house of many mansions, and there is always room, and need, for the gifted, instinctive player; as Garrincha, in that very World Cup, was to show with Brazil.

To qualify for Sweden, Ireland had to accomplish the 'impossible' feat of eliminating Italy, not to mention Portugal. The Portuguese had yet to reach their heights of the early sixties, when Benfica would produce a team to delight and dominate Europe, but they were no easy victims. As for the Italians, invertebrate though they may have shown themselves in away matches, they had the tradition of two World Cup victories behind them, and a crop of native talent laced and reinforced by *oriundi*, South American stars of Italian descent. In Rome, Ireland were obliged to put the tiny Billy

Cush, a wing-half, at centre-half, but played so well and with such spirit that they lost only by a goal.

The following Autumn, they came to Wembley and, wonder of wonders, defeated England. Harry Gregg, the Manchester United goalkeeper by the time Munich came, and a great admirer of Blanchflower, worked wonders in goal. Clearly if the Irish were capable of that, they must have felt themselves capable of anything.

As they were. Early in the New Year, they were due to play Italy in mid-week in Belfast. M. Zsolt, the Hungarian referee, was held up in the fog and didn't get there, so that the teams had to play a futile friendly, instead. This didn't please an already violently partisan crowd, which became increasingly more violent as the referee lost control, and foul succeeded foul. The limit was reached when Beppe Chiappella, the Italian right-half, jumped with both knees into the back of Billy McAdams, Ireland's centre-forward.

At the final whistle, with score 2–2, the crowd brutally invaded the pitch and attacked the Italian players. Police and the Irish players helped them to escape; it was the kind of scene to which Blanchflower himself was totally alien.

For another of his qualities was his absolute sportsmanship on the field. No doubt he committed fouls now and again, but it is hard to remember any of them. Nor can one dismiss this by saying that the really gifted player has no need to indulge in roughness. A long, long line of Scottish international wing-halves bears depressing witness to the contrary. Violence was simply remote from Blanchflower's nature, and when it was visited on him, he became understandably bitter. One of the few occasions I can recall him being really angry was when, on a train journey, he was talking of a recent match at Everton, in which he had been brutally charged down from behind, the referee looking on with indulgence. Competitive almost to a fault, his career – at a time when so many vital matches turn into brawls – reassures one that competitiveness need not always turn into cynicism and viciousness.

A few weeks later, Ireland played Italy again and this time beat them, deservedly, 2–1. It was a triumph for Blanchflower and for McIlroy, who scored one of the goals. This time, both crowd and Italians alike seemed purged of anger, so that the Irish, by and large, were able to play the pure football of which they were capable. Their victory was an appalling blow for Italy, who thus failed for the first time to reach the finals, but it was an uplifting achievement for Doherty and little Ireland.

It is notable that Blanchflower, for his behaviour after the first, savage affair, was praised by Ottorino Barassi, the Italian Vice President of F.I.F.A. It was Blanchflower who had seen to it that each Italian player had an Irish escort from the pitch, moving Barassi to remark, 'Blanchflower is a man of many parts, and a gentleman.'

At the end of the season, he was deservedly voted Footballer of the Year, an honour which would be conferred on him a second time, when captaining Spurs to their successes.

There was another absentee from the Irish team which travelled to Sweden. Or rather, Billy Simpson, the big Rangers centre-forward, though he made the trip, was too badly injured to play. So Ireland had to manufacture, from their bare resources, another centre-forward as well as a new centre-half, and though they did amazingly well in the circumstances, they did not really manage it.

They stayed at a little seaside town called Tylosand, in a hotel above the beach, with a pitch situated picturesquely in a nearby wood, to play on. The atmosphere had none of the cold formality of the England party, where every man seemed to be looking over his shoulder. Doherty, though he never lost control of his team and its players, knew how to weld them into a cheerful family – and in Blanchflower and McIlroy, he had mature lieutenants.

Their opposition was alarming; Argentina, re-entering the World Cup after long sulks and silence, Czechoslovakia – and the World Cup holders, West Germany. Clearly it would be a splendid achievement if they finished in the first two of their group, to qualify for the quarter-finals.

And they did. They beat the Czechs, they lost to the Argentinians, they drew with the West Germans, then, in a play-off, they beat the Czechs again. Finally, an exhausted and depleted team, they went down to the French, in the quarter-finals. Obliged, as we have seen, to mask his batteries, Blanchflower only came fully into his own, perhaps in the play-off against the Czechs, in Malmo. These, a few days earlier, had thrashed Argentina 6–1, and were locally the favourites against what was by now a scratch Irish side. But the wonderful morale of the Irish players carried them through. In extra time, with the score 1–1, Blanchflower floated one of his long, immaculate free kicks across the Czech goal, and McParland scored with a right-footed volley, to put the Irish, incredibly, into the final eight.

With seven injured players and the imbecility of a two hundred and ten mile coach ride to Norkopping, they had little real hope from the first. The French, thanks to the anomalies of the competition, had benefited from four days' rest, and it was clear that Ireland needed some kind of miracle. They did not get it, but if one of the ideas that Blanchflower, Bingham and McIlroy had devised had only been fully worked out, things might have been different.

For almost half the game, Jack was as good as, and better than, his master. Then the idea was put into practice, took the French by surprise – but it was not exploited. It involved a throw-in on the Irish right flank. The intention was for Blanchflower to throw the ball to Bingham, Bingham, with his head, to flick it to McIlroy, and McIlroy to run through for a shot at goal.

It worked; up to a point. Blanchflower threw in, Bingham duly headed on, and McIlroy ran into the penalty area. But instead of shooting he squared the ball across the goal, and the chance was gone. France went on to score four times, and Ireland's brave attempt had ended in anti-climax. Still, it was a superb achievement to get to Sweden at all, and an even finer one to reach the quarter-finals against such strenuous opposition.

For the future, Blanchflower's greatest triumphs were reserved for club football with the Spurs. This, now, had a more fascinating aspect than it ever had in the past, for victory in the English Cup and League meant entry into European competition, the sort of thing which was meat and drink to Blanchflower, always looking for new challenges, new approaches, fresh aspects of the game.

He had settled in a pleasant house in a North London suburb with Betty, his second wife, and their three agreeable children. His first marriage, which came to an end while he lived in Birmingham, had been to an Ulster girl – and he was to marry a third time, to a South African. On arrival in London, he had begun an amusing column for the *Evening News* which, while it did not extend him, was often humorously inventive.

In season 1960-61, Spurs began the League season with a remarkable unbeaten run, and cantered on to win the Championship. They were essentially an attacking team, highly talented, if not a great club side in the manner of Real Madrid. Blanchflower, John White and Dave Mackay were perhaps their three outstanding players, but there were also the lean, professional Bill Brown, of Scotland, in goal, and the tremendously brave Cliff Jones, on the right or left wing. Blanchflower's clever crosses into the penalty area were as well tailored for his flying headers as Alf Ramsey's had been, a decade earlier, for the headers of Leslie Medley.

Looking back, Blanchflower has said that he enjoyed playing with them all; that there was no player whom he enjoyed playing with more than any other. There were times, he added, when Jimmy McIlroy would tell him he thought he played badly for Ireland, to which Blanchflower would reply, 'You don't play badly, you just play differently.'

The Ireland team had reached its apotheosis with the 1958 World Cup. The following October, it lost at home, 5–2, to England. 'How England won 5–2 nobody knew,' Blanchflower said. 'We should have won 5–2. They were meant to have been playing 4-2-4; all they'd done was play two centre-halves to stop our two centre-forwards, and afterwards they went on like that for thirteen games.'

His account of the scene outside the England dressing-rooms, after the match, shows him at his best as a raconteur and a close observer. 'X of the *Daily* —— is very excited, this is England's greatest victory for years, and he says to Walter Winterbottom, "Walter, would you say England was playing 4-2-4?" And Walter looks up, and he doesn't find the answer up there, and he looks down again, then he looks up, and he says . . . "Yes." And——says, "What I thought was so-and-so and so-and-so. And so-and-so and so-and-so and so-and-so and so-and-so." And then Bob Pennington of the *Daily Express* comes forward with a big smile, his rival, and he says, "Thank you very much, Walter. And now do you think we can have ——'s views?" And all the little local journalists standing round, amazed at this quarrel between the big boys! '

Spurs won the 1960-61 Championship with a forward-line led by the powerful Bobby Smith, with Les Allen an excellent, incisive inside-left. The following December, however, they paid some £99,000 to buy Jimmy Greaves from Milan, so that Blanchflower was captaining a still more richly gifted side. At that time, he feels, Spurs and Benfica, the holders of the European Cup, were the two best club teams in Europe, Real Madrid having passed their zenith.

The two clubs met in the quarter-finals, and Benfica got home by a goal. Blanchflower thinks that Spurs had two and possibly three good goals disallowed for offside, the first two in Lisbon – particularly one by Bobby Smith – the other by Jimmy Greaves, early in an exciting match at White Hart Lane. Spurs won it, hectically, by the odd goal, but it wasn't enough to keep them in.

Intriguingly, Blanchflower endorses the fast and physical nature of Tottenham's football in the second leg, although it was very much in the image of Mackay, rather than his own. Many of us criticised Tottenham for their methods; it is significant that Blanchflower, though they were so foreign to his own approach, should still feel they were right. 'It wasn't football,' he has said, 'but that was what was needed. If a team came out to play defensive football, the very thing it wanted was for the other side to play a rational, cool, elaborate game.' Others might think that pressure defeats itself, that the modern game has, for the last forty years, been built on the sudden breakaway, but Blanchflower's view is an interesting one.

He scored from a penalty-kick in that game; cool enough, as usual, to make a very good job of it, selling the excellent Costa Pereira, in goal, a dummy, then sliding the ball into the left hand corner, after Pereira himself had moved left. Afterwards, Pereira told him that it was the first time anybody had sent him the wrong way. This penalty-kick had an interesting sequel, for a few months later, at Wembley, during the Cup Final, Blanchflower was called upon to take another one, against Burnley.

He was so convinced that Adam Blacklaw, Burnley's Scottish goalkeeper, would have seen his penalty against Benfica on television that he decided to try to send him the other way from Pereira. As he walked up to take the kick, Jimmy McIlroy, who 'used to take them for Ireland, and miss them, said to me, "You're going to miss it." I said, "I'm glad *you're* not taking it." ' And Blanchflower did not miss it. He duly sent Blacklaw to the left, and put the ball in, to the right.

The following season, he and Spurs had consolation, when they thrashed Atletico Madrid 5–1 in Rotterdam, to win the Final of the European Cupwinners' Cup. By this time, Blanchflower was 'assistant to the manager, whatever that meant,' and on the morning of the game, Billy Nicholson decreed that there should be training. The team, already demoralised by its poor form over the past six weeks, resented this; all the talk was of bonuses; of who would and who would not be playing.

'I'd been playing terrible,' Blanchflower said, 'because unconsciously I was carrying my knee. I told them, "You're all afraid of this match. I deserve to play more than anybody and I don't know if I'm playing, and I'm not worrying. I'm going out to train. If you're not training, please yourselves; you can sit and play cards, if you like." ' The players trained – and they won.

From this, it can be deduced that Blanchflower might have become an exceptional manager yet, while playing, he always denied any ambition to do so. He had, he said, been disappointed too often and one cannot imagine him suffering directors gladly. Even at Tottenham, where things had certainly improved since the fifties, 'I said that the team at Tottenham was bigger than the club, when I left. I felt that Tottenham never made the best of those years.' It may also be that Blanchflower was too much the individualist, even the egoist, to have submitted to the grinding compromises of management. Shrewd about the psychology of footballers – I remember his once saying of a successful manager, 'X hasn't done anything. He's just sat there and sucked his pipe and given them confidence' – one nevertheless sees him as a lone wolf, impatient of stupidity.

He had by now become a 'fashionable' figure, taken up by such as Professor Ayer, the logical positivist philosopher, author of *Language, Truth and Logic,* whom Blanchflower once reproached on a television programme for being superstitious, and Karl Miller, the young literary editor, then, of the *New Statesman.* Blanchflower wrote frequently for the *New Statesman,* sometimes very well, and later had a fruitful period on the *Observer.* One has always felt it a pity he left them to spread himself over the wider but less exacting spaces of the *Sunday Express,* for he seemed to have there the direction and discipline his writing demands. It is hard for a footballer who has, as Blanchflower admits, been 'adulated,' and has reached such peaks, to buckle down to the needs of another *métier*; yet just as the tension between his own talent and the demands of organisation probably brought the best out of him as a footballer, so a similar tension might bring the best out of him as a writer. A tendency to sentimentality, mild vendetta and a sacrifice of individuality to the fashions of American sports journalism might thus have been avoided.

Not surprisingly, perhaps, his admirations in literature have tended towards the romantic, in particular to Scott Fitzgerald, that doomed, gilded, perennial adolescent of the protracted nineteen-twenties. Though he writes, now, for the popular Press, his relations with it have long been uneasy; one remembers a ferocious *New Statesman* column, after the World Cup finals of 1962, in Chile, which presumed that one writer must have come home to be sick into his well advertised bowler hat. Misquotation, malice and the cynical kite flying which he so often met during his playing career were not likely to be received by him with tolerance.

Despite the breadth of his interest, he testifies to the shock of leaving football; which he did, at last, in 1964. 'There's a strange awakening when you come out of the game, because we're all very spoiled in the game. You've had so much adulation. You've spent ten years having things done for you, Army style.'

Retiring, he embarked, with bright success, on television as well as journalism, and in 1967, became one of the commentators on the C.B.S. network of the first professional soccer league to be played in the United States. Beyond question one of the great footballers of his day, a great captain in an age when captaincy was moribund if not dead, his major contribution, perhaps, was to give the professional footballer a rational, articulate voice.